SECOND EDITION

TOP NOTCH FUNDAMENTALS

Workbook

Joan Saslow • Allen Ascher

With Julie C. Rouse

Top Notch: English for Today's World Fundamentals, Second Edition
Workbook

Pearson Education, 10 Bank Street, White Plains, NY 10606

Staff credits: The people who made up the *Top Notch Fundamentals Workbook* team, representing editorial, design, production, and manufacturing, are Rhea Banker, Elizabeth Carlson, Aerin Csigay, Mindy DePalma, Dave Dickey, Aliza Greenblatt, Ray Keating, Mike Kemper, Jessica Miller-Smith, and Barbara Sabella.

Cover design: Rhea Banker
Cover photo: Sprint/Corbis
Text design: Wendy Wolf
Text composition: Quarasan!
Text font: ITC Stone Sans

Photo credits: All original photography by David Mager. Page 1 (1) Cat Gwynn/Getty Images, (2) Shutterstock.com, (3) Shutterstock.com, (4) Shutterstock.com; p. 2 (top) Courtesy of Korean Concert Society, (bottom) AP Images/Petr David Josek; p. 4 (left) Steve Finn/Getty Images, (right) Frank Micelotta/Getty Images; p. 5 (left) Shutterstock.com, (middle left) Mark Richards/PhotoEdit Inc., (middle right) Shutterstock.com, (right) Shutterstock.com; p. 13 (top) Shutterstock.com, (bottom) Jeff Greenberg/PhotoEdit Inc.; p. 15 (top) Shutterstock.com, (middle top) Shutterstock.com, (middle bottom) Jeff Greenberg/PhotoEdit Inc., (bottom) Shutterstock.com; p. 18 (1) Tim Graham/Corbis, (2) Corbis, (3) Shutterstock.com, (4) Tim Graham/Corbis, (5) Tim Graham/Corbis; p. 43 (top) Reuters/Corbis, (bottom left) Bettmann/Corbis, (bottom right) Miramax/Dimension Films/The Kobal Collection; p. 44 (1) Picture Quest/Jim Pickerell/Stock Connection, (2) Keith Brofsky/Getty Images, (3) Royalty-Free/Corbis, (4) Shutterstock.com, (5) Shutterstock.com, (6) Shutterstock.com; p. 45 (top middle) Shutterstock.com, (top right) Shutterstock.com, (bottom left) Shutterstock.com, (bottom middle) Tom & Dee Ann McCarthy/Corbis, (bottom right) Corbis; p. 46 (1) Shutterstock.com; p. 47 (3) Shutterstock.com, (4) Shutterstock.com, (5) Shutterstock.com, (middle left) Robert Brenner/PhotoEdit, Inc., (middle right) Shutterstock.com, (bottom right) Shutterstock.com; p. 48 (1) Shutterstock.com, (2) Shutterstock.com, (3) Photolibrary.com; p. 49 (4) Shutterstock.com, (5) Scott Van Dyke/Beateworks/Corbis, (6) AP Images/Julie Jacobson; p. 51 (left) Randy Faris/Corbis, (right) Dallas and John Heaton/Corbis; p. 62 Comstock Images; p. 68 (top left) Graham French/Masterfile, (top left inset) Original Films/The Kobal Collection, (top middle) Shutterstock.com, (middle left) Shutterstock.com, (middle right) Shutterstock.com, (bottom) Shutterstock.com; p. 73 Shutterstock.com; p. 83 AFP/Corbis; p. 85 AP Images; p. 90 Shutterstock.com.

Illustration credits: Steve Attoe: pages 2, 26 (bottom), 80; Kenneth Batelman: page 17; Leanne Franson: pages 3, 7, 20, 25, 49; Scott Fray: page 59; Brian Hughes: page 84; Steve Hutchings: pages 37, 55, 62; Suzanne Mogensen: pages 21, 26, 59, 79; Dusan Petriçic: pages 1, 26 (top), 31, 34, 47, 53 (top), 54 (bottom), 67, 87 (center, right); Michelle Rabagliati: pages 31 (bottom), 32 (bottom); Phil Scheuer: pages 53 (bottom), 54 (top), 73, 77, 85, 86, 87 (left); Steve Schulman: pages 32, 33 (bottom), 41; Jessica Miller-Smith: page 71; Neil Stewart: pages 13, 15, 18, 28 (bottom), 40, 48; Anna Veltfort: pages 8, 53 (bottom), 66, 77; Patrick Welsh: pages 14 (top), 25 (top-right, top-left).

ISBN 13: 978-0-13-246991-3
ISBN 10: 0-13-246991-X

Printed in the United States of America
1 2 3 4 5 6 7 8 9 10–V042–15 14 13 12 11 10

CONTENTS

UNIT 1

Names and Occupations

LESSON 1

Match the occupations with the pictures. Write the letter on the line.

1. ____ a teacher
2. ____ an artist
3. ____ an athlete
4. ____ a musician
5. ____ a flight attendant
6. ____ a banker
7. ____ a singer

a. 

b. 

c. 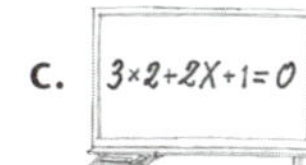

d. 

e. 

f. 

g. 

2 FAMOUS PEOPLE. **What are their occupations? Write sentences. Use contractions.**

1. Frank Gehry: *He's an architect* ______________________________.
2. Lance Armstrong: ______________________________.
3. Shakira: ______________________________.
4. Matt Damon: ______________________________.

3 **Complete the conversation between Hee-Young Lim and Constantina Tomescu.**

Hee-Young Lim: Hi. I'm Hee-Young.

Constantina Tomescu: Hi, ______________________________.

Hee-Young Lim: Nice to meet you, Constantina.

Constantina Tomescu: ______________________________.

Hee-Young Lim: What do you do?

Constantina Tomescu: ______________________________.

______________________________?

Hee-Young Lim: I'm a musician.

LESSON 2

4 **Match the occupations that go together. Write the letter on the line.**

1. __c__ a singer
2. _____ a teacher
3. _____ an architect
4. _____ a pilot

a. a student
b. a flight attendant
c. a musician
d. an engineer

5 **Circle the occupation that is different.**

1. scientist	engineer	chef	doctor
2. singer	manager	actor	athlete
3. banker	artist	musician	photographer

6 **Look at the people going to work. Write sentences about their occupations. Use contractions.**

1. She's an artist.
2. ______________________________.
3. ______________________________.
4. ______________________________.
5. ______________________________.
6. ______________________________.

7 Complete the sentences with names.

1. My favorite singer is ______________________.
2. My favorite actor is ______________________.
3. My favorite athlete is ______________________.
4. ______________________ is a famous artist.
5. ______________________ is a famous musician.
6. ______________________ is a famous writer.

8 Read the list. Then look at the pictures and complete the conversations.

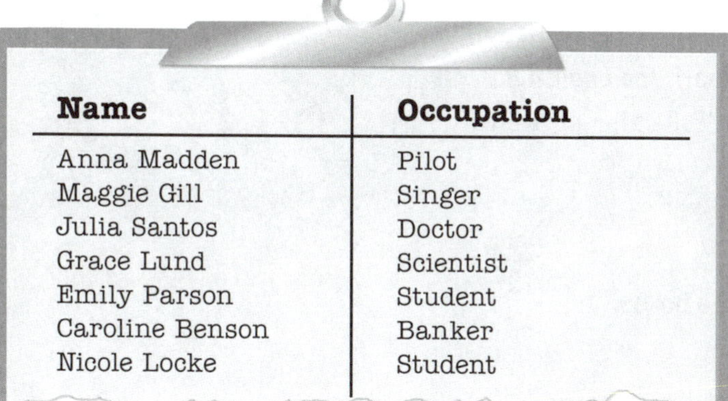

Name	Occupation
Anna Madden	Pilot
Maggie Gill	Singer
Julia Santos	Doctor
Grace Lund	Scientist
Emily Parson	Student
Caroline Benson	Banker
Nicole Locke	Student

Are you Maggie?

1. *No, I'm not.*
I'm Grace.

Are you Anna?

2. ______________________
____

Are you Caroline?

3. ______________________
____

Are you Emily and Nicole?

4. ______________________
____

9 Read about Madonna.

Madonna is a famous singer. She's also an actor. And she's a writer, too. Three occupations! The name of her first children's book is *The English Roses*. Madonna is the writer, but she's not the artist. The artist is Jeffrey Fulvimari. *The English Roses* is now a collection of twelve books.

Now answer the questions. Check ✔ the boxes.

1. What are Madonna's occupations?

☐ artist	☐ photographer	☐ teacher
☐ actor	☐ singer	☐ writer

2. What is Jeffrey Fulvimari's occupation?

☐ writer	☐ actor	☐ artist

10 Circle the occupation that is not spelled correctly.

1.	engineer	doctor	arkitect	athlete
2.	shef	banker	teacher	singer
3.	scientist	fotographer	musician	manager
4.	writer	pilot	actor	flite attendant

Now write the words correctly.

5. ______________________________
6. ______________________________
7. ______________________________
8. ______________________________

LESSON 3

11 **Rewrite the sentences. Capitalize the proper nouns.**

1. john landry is a chef in paris.

   ______________________________.

2. isabel hunter is from canada. She's an architect.

   ______________________________.

3. alex quinn is a pilot. He's in tokyo today.

   ______________________________.

12 **Write proper and common nouns. Capitalize the proper nouns.**

1. Your name: ______________
2. Your occupation: ______________
3. Your teacher's name: ______________
4. Matt Damon's occupation: ______________

13 **Read the occupations in the box. Count the syllables. Write each occupation in the correct place on the chart.**

athlete	chef	~~engineer~~	actor	manager
musician	photographer	scientist	singer	writer

1 syllable	2 syllables	3 syllables	4 syllables
		engineer	

14 **Choose the correct response. Circle the letter.**

1. How are you?
   a. I'm Samantha. **b.** Great. **c.** Take care.
2. What do you do?
   a. I'm a manager. **b.** Fine, thanks. **c.** I'm Jim.
3. Are you Lucy?
   a. Yes, she is. **b.** OK. See you! **c.** No, I'm not.
4. How do you spell that?
   a. Right over there. **b.** T-O-M-E-S-C-U. **c.** I'm a writer. And you?

JUST FOR **FUN**

A RIDDLE FOR YOU!

Ms. Adams, Ms. Banks, Ms. Clark, and Ms. Dare have four different occupations—**engineer, architect, doctor,** and **scientist** (but NOT in that order).

Read the statements.

Ms. Adams and Ms. Clark are not doctors.

Ms. Banks and Ms. Clark are not scientists.

Ms. Clark and Ms. Dare are not architects.

Ms. Adams is not a scientist.

Now write an occupation for each person.

Ms. Adams: ____________________

Ms. Banks: ____________________

Ms. Clark: ____________________

Ms. Dare: ____________________

Source: Adapted from norfolkacademy.org.

2 WORD FIND. Look across (→) and down (↓). Circle the eight occupations. Then write the occupations on the lines.

____

____

____

____

____

____

____

____

N E I M E P A E N N B K R P P E
M O E T E O A M E S U I H A T L
A E L P O L L H N C N N N T R Y
N T W E S A A S A I H H R R L I
A O R H T E T T R E T E T E N C
G K I E N P H E S N A H N E S A
E N T P C R L A M T R E N S R E
R T E A E A E I N I N N E R N U
K A R A S H T A A S E R E R A T
O A T N Y T E I U T E H G R N M
E C P H O T O G R A P H E R H E
R T N A S M B E N G I N E E R B
N O E N R A E E E E R A E R E L
A R O K P E G N E R A N U U H E
O T T B A N K E R T L E G C T E
N N K R N N E R N R T B I G E T

Source: Created with spellbuilder.com.

Riddle: Ms. Adams: architect; Ms. Banks: doctor; Ms. Clark: engineer; Ms. Dare: scientist

UNIT 2

About People

LESSON 1

Look at the pictures. Write possessive adjectives.

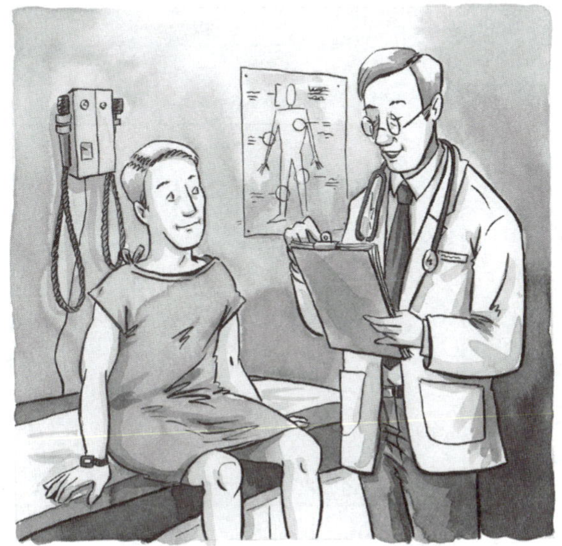

1. His doctor is Dr. Brown.

2. _________ teacher is Ms. Jalbert.

3. _________ boss is Mr. Lin.

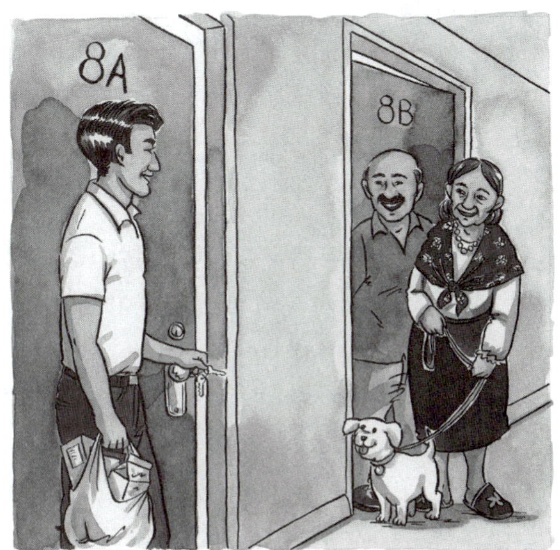

4. _________ neighbors are Mr. and Mrs. Rivers.

2 Look at the pictures. Complete the sentences about relationships. Use possessive nouns.

1. He is *Eric's classmate* ____________.

2. She is ____________.

3. They are ____________.

4. He is ____________.

3 Complete the sentences.

1. Audrey is ________ (I / my) classmate.
2. We're ________ (Mr. Haber's / Mr. Haber) students.
3. Who is ________ (you / your) manager?
4. Ms. Miller and Mr. Sullivan are ________ (our / we) colleagues.
5. Are ________ (they / their) your neighbors?
6. Dr. Franklin isn't ________ (Bill / Bill's) doctor.

4 Match the description and the relationship. Write the letter on the line.

1. _____ Caleb and I are managers. Our company is Infotech. Our boss is Mr. Jackson.
2. _____ Anna's address is 32 Arbor Street. Zoe's address is 34 Arbor Street.
3. _____ Ryan and Josh are students in the same class. Ms. Foster is their teacher.
4. _____ Jessica and I are classmates. She's my neighbor, too.

a. They're classmates.
b. We're colleagues.
c. They're neighbors.
d. We're friends.

5 **Look at Joe's list and Amy's list for their party.**

JOE'S LIST

Kristin – friend
Jeff – friend
Robert and Julie – friends
Mark – classmate
Gary and Ann – neighbors

Amy's List

Samantha – colleague
Peter – colleague
Katherine – boss
Gary and Ann – neighbors
Robert and Julie – friends

Now write sentences about the people. Use possessive adjectives.

1. Peter: *Peter is her colleague* ________.
2. Mark: ________.
3. Gary and Ann: ________.
4. Katherine: ________.
5. Kristin: ________.

6 **YOUR RELATIONSHIPS. Complete the chart with names.**

Classmates or Colleagues	Neighbors	Friends

7 **Choose a friend and a classmate from Exercise 6. Introduce them. Complete the conversation.**

1. **You:** ________, this is ________.
   ________'s my classmate.
2. **Your friend:** Hi, ________.
3. **Your classmate:** Hi, ________. Nice to meet you.
   Your friend: Nice to meet you, too.
   Your classmate: What do you do?
4. **Your friend:** I'm ________. And you?
5. **Your classmate:** I'm ________.
   Your friend: Where are you from?
6. **Your classmate:** I'm from ________.

LESSON 2

8 **Fill out the form for a friend, a neighbor, or a colleague.**

☐ Mr.
☐ Mrs. ______________ ______________
☐ Miss *first name* *last name*
☐ Ms.

Now complete the conversation between the person and a clerk.

1. **Clerk:** Hi. What's your last name, please?
   __________: ______________________________________.
2. **Clerk:** And your first name?
   __________: My first name? ______________________________.
3. **Clerk:** How do you spell that?
   __________: ______________________________________.
4. **Clerk:** Thank you.
   __________: ______________________________________.

9 **Complete the sentences. Use real names and relationships.**

1. Mr. ______________ is my ______________.
2. Mr. and Mrs. ______________ are my ______________.
3. Ms. ______________ is my ______________.
4. Miss ______________ is my ______________.

LESSON 3

10 **Complete the address book with information for three friends.**

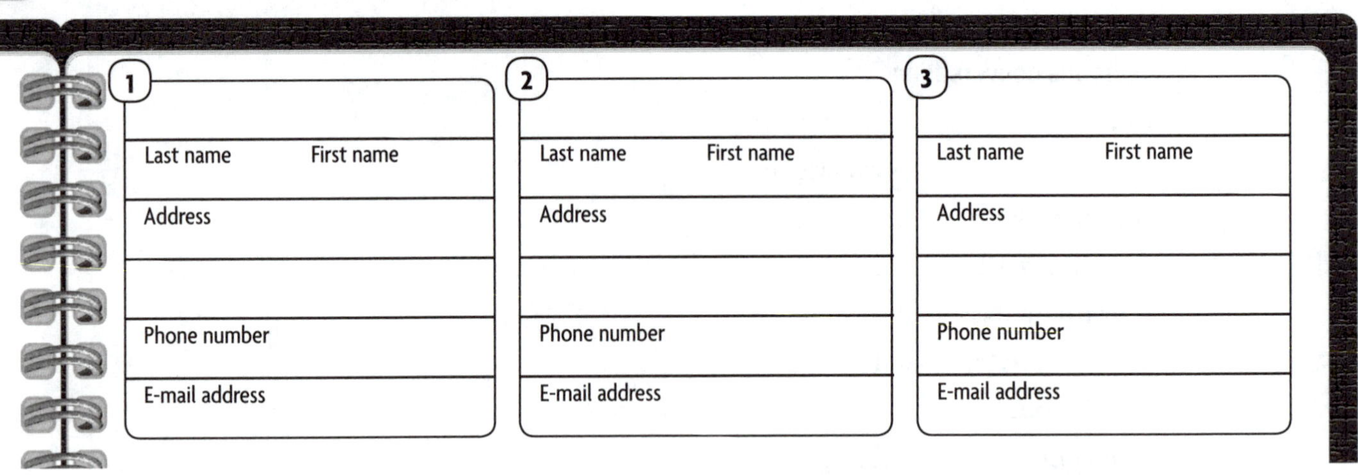

11 **Write the answers in words.**

1. eleven + six = ______________________
2. nineteen – twelve = ______________________
3. three x five = ______________________
4. twenty ÷ two = ______________________

12 **Look at the business cards. Read the responses. Then write questions with <u>What's</u>. Use possessive nouns or possessive adjectives.**

1. A: What's Ms. Harrison's first name? B: Kate.
2. A: What's her address? B: 77 York St.
3. A: ______________________? B: jeff.silver@edi.com
4. A: ______________________? B: He's a manager.
5. A: ______________________? B: 0208 755 8050.
6. A: ______________________? B: 28 Manor Street.

13 **Answer the questions. Use your own information.**

1. What's your first name? ______________________.
2. What's your last name? ______________________.
3. What's your occupation? ______________________.
4. What's your address? ______________________.
5. What's your phone number? ______________________.
6. What's your e-mail address? ______________________.

JUST FOR **FUN**

1 TAKE A GUESS! Write the next number in words.

1. three, six, nine, twelve, fifteen, ________________
2. one, two, four, eight, ________________
3. twenty, one, nineteen, two, eighteen, three, ________________

Source: From riddlenut.com.

2 Complete the puzzle.

Across

4. We are _____. Our addresses are 15 and 17 Pine Street.
5. The Musee du Louvre's _____ is 99 Rue de Rivoli, Paris.
9. Frank Gehry's occupation
10. Her name is Linda Reid. Reid is her _____ name.

Down

1. Mr. Bryant is Andy's teacher. Andy is _____ student.
2. Their address is 11 Palm Street, and their _____ is (661) 555–4485.
3. Banana Yoshimoto's title
6. Allison's _____ address is allie@mail.net.
7. Flight attendants and pilots are _____.
8. A=one, B=two, C=three, . . . N= _____

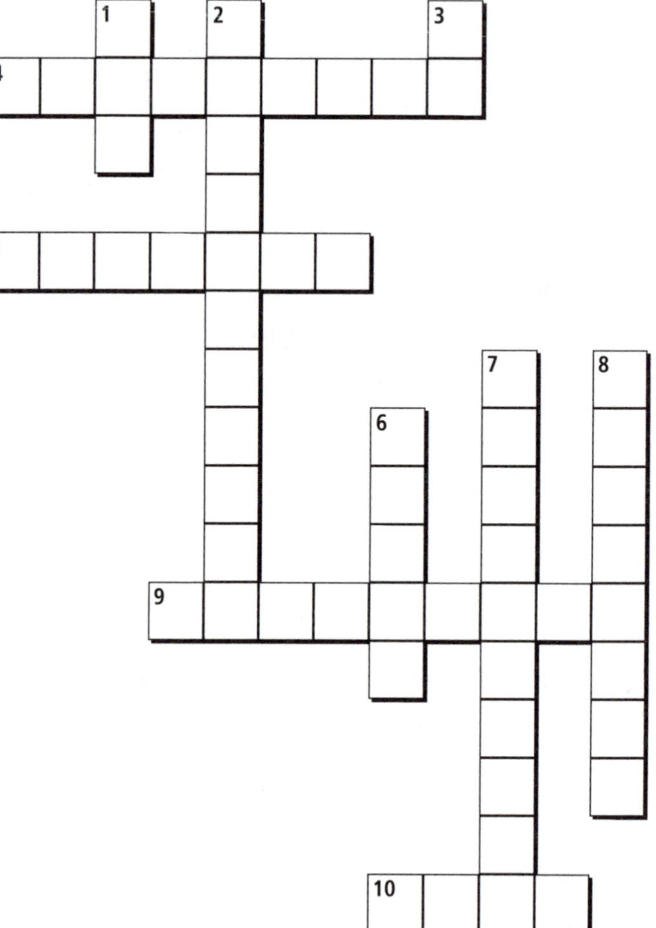

Source: Created with Discovery's Puzzlemaker.

Guess: 1. eighteen; 2. sixteen; 3. seventeen

UNIT 3

Places and How to Get There

LESSON 1

1 **Write the names of places in your neighborhood.**

1. a restaurant: ______________________
2. a bank: ______________________
3. a bookstore: ______________________
4. a pharmacy: ______________________
5. a school: ______________________

2 **Read the directions. Label the places on the map.**

- The school is across the street.
- The bookstore is around the corner.
- The bank is next to the bookstore.
- The newsstand is down the street on the left.
- The pharmacy is down the street on the right.

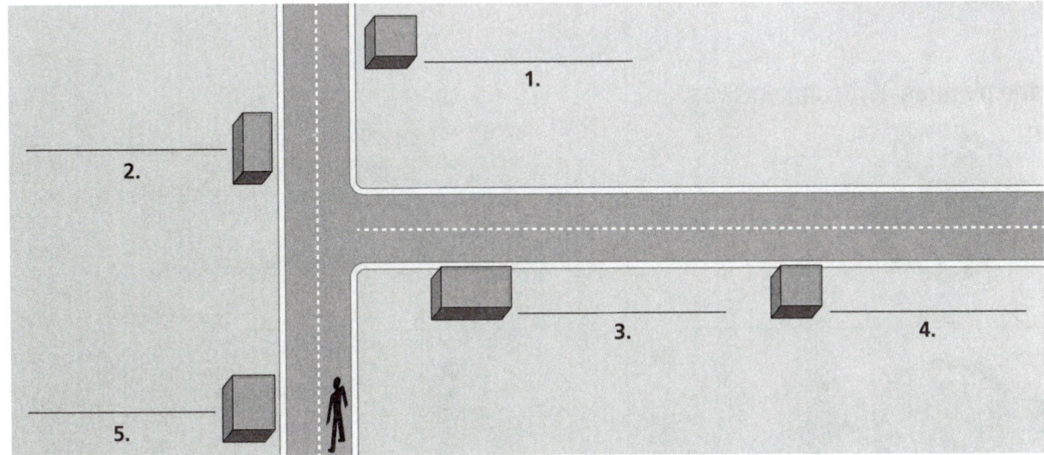

3 **Read the answers. Then complete the questions with Where's or What's.**

1. A: __________ the address? B: 214 New Street.
2. A: __________ the bookstore? B: It's down the street on the left.
3. A: __________ the pharmacy? B: It's across the street.
4. A: __________ Lisa's occupation? B: She's a photographer.
5. A: __________ his e-mail address? B: Rob123@mail.net.
6. A: __________ your friend's restaurant? B: It's around the corner.

4 Look at the pictures. Write questions and answers. Follow the model.

1. 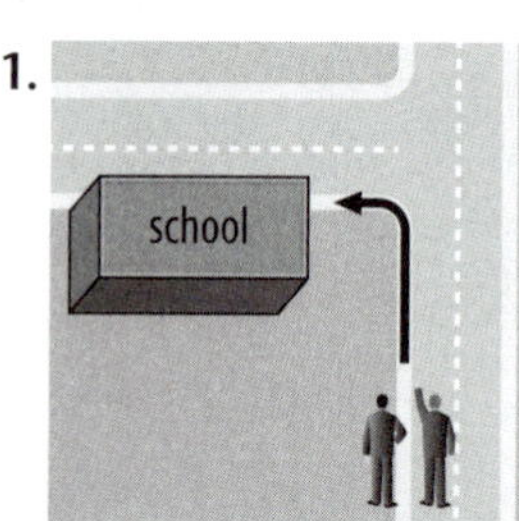

2. 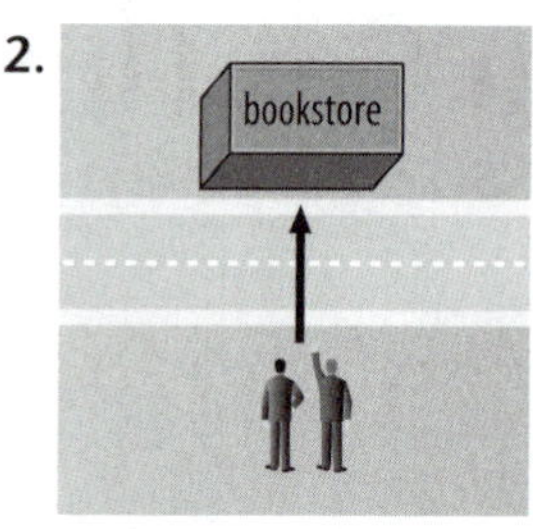

3. 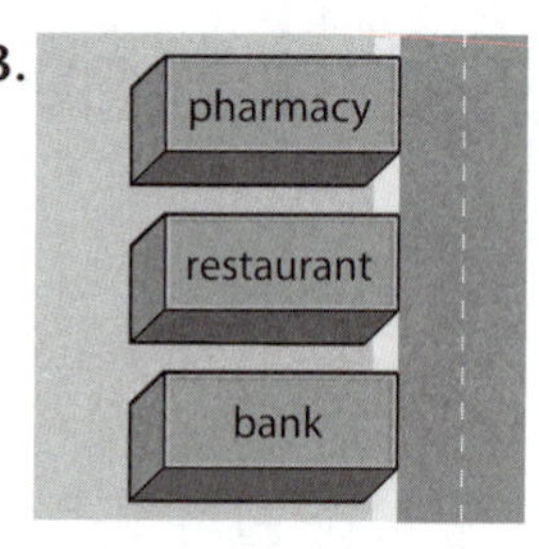

4. 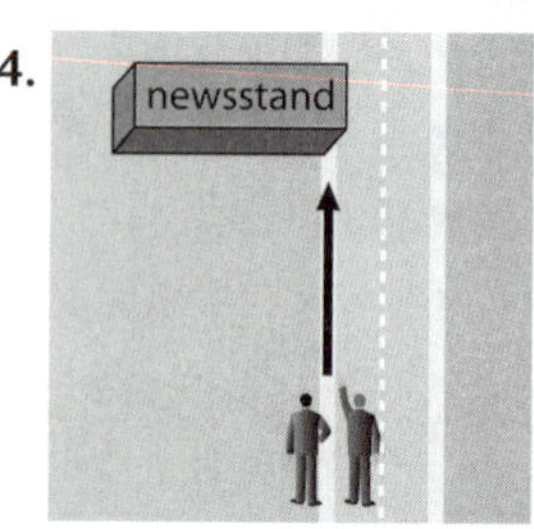

1. A: Where's the school? B: It's around the corner.
2. A: ____________________? B: ____________________.
3. A: ____________________? B: ____________________.
4. A: ____________________? B: ____________________.

LESSON 2

5 Complete the conversation. Tell a friend how to get to your school.

1. **Your friend:** Can I walk to the school?
   YOU ____________________.
2. **Your friend:** OK. And where is it?
   YOU ____________________.
3. **Your friend:** OK. Thanks!
   YOU ____________________.

6 Look at the pictures. Write imperatives.

1. Don't drive.

2. ____________________.

3. ____________________.

4. ____________________.

5. ____________________.

7 Tell a new classmate how to go places from school. Use an affirmative and a negative imperative.

Example: to a bookstore: Take the bus. Don't walk.

1. to a bookstore: ______________________
2. to a bank: ______________________
3. to a pharmacy: ______________________
4. to a restaurant: ______________________

8 Look at the pictures. Write a sentence with an imperative and a sentence about the location. Follow the model.

1. 

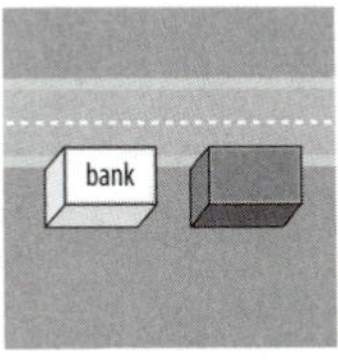

Take a taxi to the bookstore.

It's next to the bank.

2.   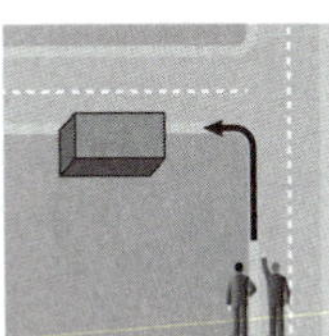

______________________.

______________________.

3.   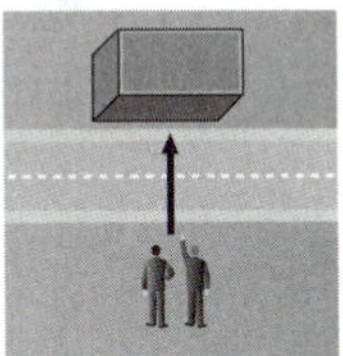

______________________.

______________________.

4.   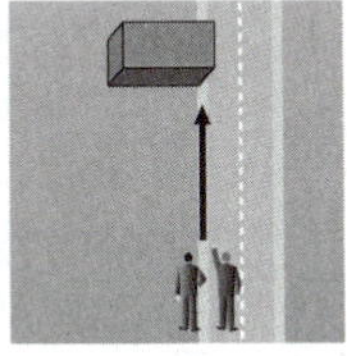

______________________.

______________________.

9 Look at the pictures. Write questions. Follow the model.

1. Can I walk to the bookstore?

2. _______________?

3. _______________?

4. _______________?

LESSON 3

10 Look at the pictures. Answer the questions. Use a by phrase.

1. How does she go home?
   By subway.

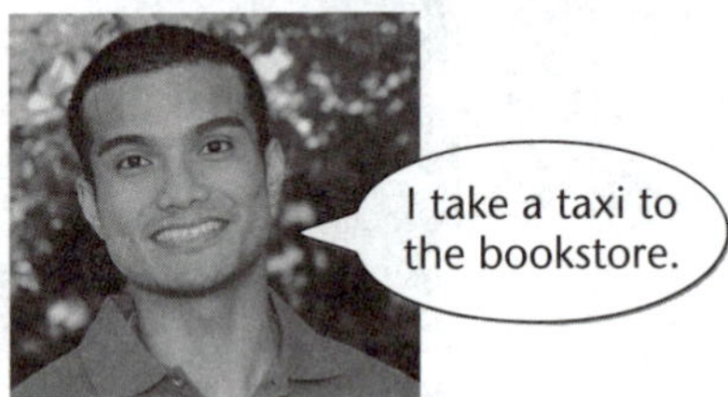

2. How does he go to the bookstore?
   _______________.

3. How do they go to work?
   _______________.

4. How does she go to school?
   _______________.

11 How do you go places? Read the sentences. Write T for sentences that are true for you and F for sentences that are false for you.

1. _____ I go to school by bicycle.
2. _____ I take a taxi to restaurants.
3. _____ I go to work by train.
4. _____ I go home from school by bus.
5. _____ I walk to the bookstore.
6. _____ I go to work by moped.
7. _____ I take the subway to the bank.

JUST FOR **FUN**

1 A RIDDLE FOR YOU! **Read the clues. Then write the places on the lines.**

- The bookstore is between the restaurant and the pharmacy.
- The bank is not next to the bookstore.
- The restaurant is next to the bank.
- The pharmacy is not on the left.

1. ____________________
2. ____________________
3. ____________________
4. ____________________

2 WORD FIND. **Look across(→) and down (↓). Circle the eight means of transportation. Then write the means of transportation on the lines.**

____

____

____

____

____

____

____

____

C	U	S	O	G	Z	Z	S	H	Z	Z	F	B	M	H
H	S	H	P	R	F	A	I	A	L	J	S	I	B	I
E	U	P	H	S	I	R	Y	T	O	X	X	S	W	S
K	B	A	N	M	O	T	O	R	C	Y	C	L	E	C
G	W	A	B	O	W	M	T	A	J	W	F	F	F	X
U	A	C	N	P	Z	P	L	I	Q	I	Y	M	F	Y
T	Y	N	C	E	S	P	I	N	B	O	Y	G	T	H
Z	M	Y	K	D	C	I	A	S	O	A	K	B	N	T
R	W	E	N	M	B	W	M	N	H	T	F	I	X	E
T	I	Y	T	L	Q	Q	E	P	O	R	U	C	P	Q
Z	A	I	U	U	R	T	S	T	A	X	I	Y	S	W
E	G	A	K	K	L	R	H	K	B	U	S	C	H	S
X	K	U	K	M	U	N	C	A	R	G	T	L	H	Z
M	J	F	N	J	R	Q	W	G	V	F	B	E	X	Y
S	C	X	T	A	U	E	O	B	Q	W	S	V	B	P

SOURCE: Created with tools.atozteacherstuff.com

Riddle: 1. bank; 2. restaurant; 3. bookstore; 4. pharmacy

UNIT 4

Family

LESSON 1

1 THE BRITISH ROYAL FAMILY. **Write the family member's relationship to Queen Elizabeth on the line.**

2 **Look at Queen Elizabeth's family again. Complete the sentences.**

1. Prince Harry is Prince William's ______.
2. Princess Anne is Zara Phillips's ______.
3. Queen Elizabeth and Prince Philip are Prince Charles's ______.
4. Prince Philip is Prince Harry's ______.
5. Queen Elizabeth is Prince Philip's ______.
6. Prince William and Prince Harry are Prince Charles's ______.
7. Prince Andrew is Princess Eugenie's ______.
8. Queen Elizabeth is Peter Phillips's ______.
9. Princess Eugenie is Princess Beatrice's ______.
10. William, Harry, Peter, Zara, Beatrice, Eugenie, and Louise are Queen Elizabeth's ______.

3 Complete the conversation. Write What, Where, or Who.

1. **Andrew:** ______________'s that?
   Hannah: That's my brother.
2. **Andrew:** ______________'s your brother's first name?
   Hannah: Paul.
3. **Andrew:** ______________'s your sister?
   Hannah: She's right there, on the left.
4. **Andrew:** ______________'s that?
   Hannah: My grandmother.
5. **Andrew:** ______________ her last name?
   Hannah: Connor.
6. **Andrew:** ______________ are your parents?
   Hannah: They're here, next to my grandmother.

4 Read the answers. Then write questions with Who.

1. **A:** ______________________________?
   B: They're my brothers.
2. **A:** ______________________________?
   B: That's my husband.
3. **A:** ______________________________?
   B: He's my father.
4. **A:** ______________________________?
   B: They're my grandparents.
5. **A:** ______________________________?
   B: She's my sister.

5 Answer the questions.

1. Who are you? ______________________________.
2. Who's your teacher? ______________________________.
3. Who are your classmates? (Name three.) ______________________________.

LESSON 2

6 Write the names of three relatives, friends, neighbors, or classmates. Then complete the chart.

Name	Relationship	Age	Occupation	pretty	handsome	cute	short	tall	old	young
Michelle	sister	26	manager	✓				✓		✓

7 Unscramble the words. Write sentences.

1. brother / tall / is / My / very ____________________.
2. handsome, / He / too / very / is ____________________.
3. your / Are / pretty / sisters ____________________?
4. is / daughter / young / Her ____________________.
5. cute / so / is / She ____________________!

8 Describe your relatives. Write sentences.

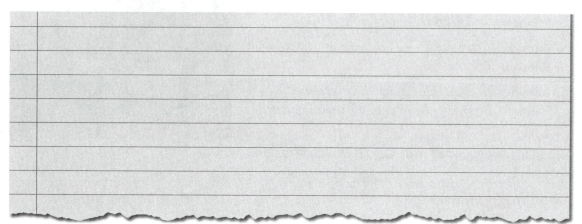

LESSON 3

9 Look at the photos and read.

Hi, I'm Kate. There are five people in my family. I have two sisters. Their names are Megan and Jane. Jane and I are students. Megan is a doctor.

Hello. My name is Edgar. My wife's name is Anna. I'm an engineer, and she's an architect. We have two children. Riley is our son, and Reese is our daughter.

Hello. I'm George. My wife Carol and I are grandparents. We have three children and two grandchildren. Our granddaughter is Sophia. Our grandson is Jake.

Now answer the questions.

1. Who's Jake? *He's George's grandson*.
2. Who's Anna? ____________________.
3. Who's Jane? ____________________.
4. Who are Riley and Reese? ____________________.
5. Who are George and Carol? ____________________.
6. Who's a doctor? ____________________.

10 Look at the picture. Write sentences with have or has.

1. Julia: She has two brothers.
2. Rose: ______.
3. Barbara and Martin: ______.
4. Dan and Michael: ______.
5. Louis: ______.

11 Write the next number in words.

1. twenty-one, twenty-eight, thirty-five, forty-two, ______
2. four, eight, sixteen, ______, sixty-four
3. ninety-nine, ______, seventy-five, sixty-three, fifty-one
4. ten, eleven, twenty-one, thirty-two, fifty-three, ______

12 Complete each sentence with have or has. Then choose the correct response. Circle the letter.

1. Matthew ______ two sisters.
   a. How old is she? b. How old are they?
2. Mark and Jamie ______ a daughter.
   a. How old is he? b. How old is she?
3. I ______ a brother and a sister.
   a. How old is your brother? b. How old is my sister?
4. We ______ a son.
   a. What's your name? b. What's his name?

1 **A RIDDLE FOR YOU! Read the sentence. Then answer the question.**

Brothers and sisters have I none, but that man's father is my father's son.

Who is "that man"? ______________

Source: From thinks.com.

2 **Complete the puzzle.**

Across

3. Julie's grandmother is ninety-five. She's _____.
6. Sons and daughters
7. A good-looking woman is _____.
8. Not tall
10. Her grandchildren are very _____. They're one and three years old.
11. A good-looking man is _____.

Down

1. The English alphabet has _____ letters.
2. My father's mother is my _____.
4. Abigail Breslin's occupation
5. His daughter's son is his _____.
7. Mother and father
9. Joan Lin is Jackie Chan's _____.

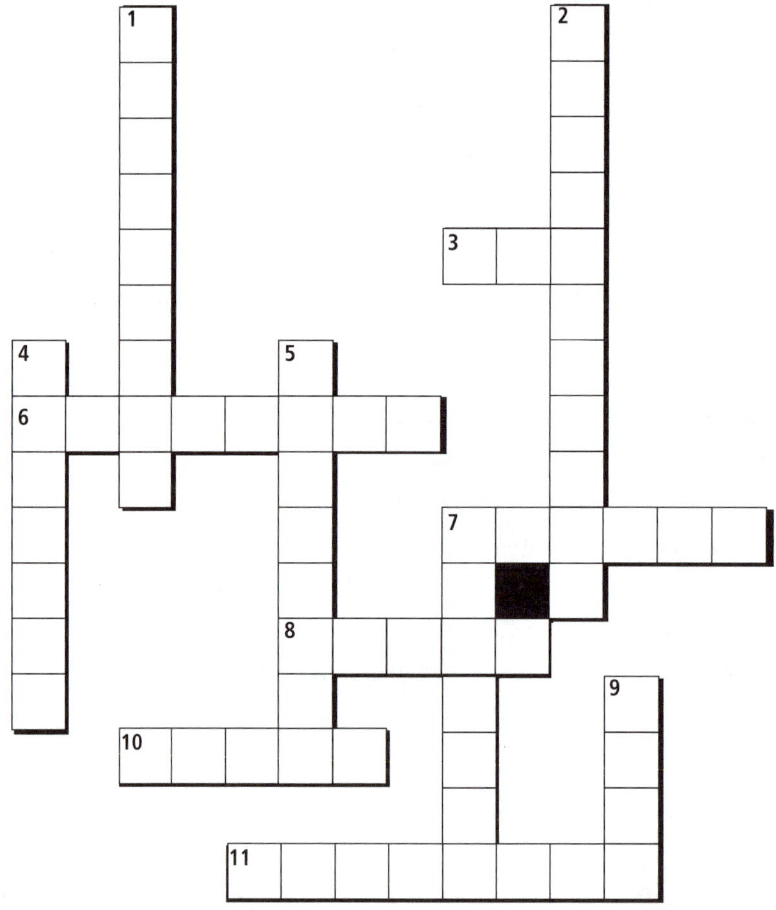

Source: Created with Discovery's Puzzlemaker.

Riddle: My son

UNIT 5

Events and Times

LESSON 1

1 **Match the times.**

1. __c__ It's half past ten. a. 6:45
2. ____ It's four o'clock. b. 8:55
3. ____ It's noon. c. 10:30
4. ____ It's a quarter after two. d. 12:00 P.M.
5. ____ It's five to nine. e. 4:00
6. ____ It's six ten. f. 6:10
7. ____ It's a quarter to seven. g. 12:00 A.M.
8. ____ It's midnight. h. 2:15

2 **Look at the pictures. Are the people <u>early</u>, <u>late</u>, or <u>on time</u>? Write sentences.**

1. ____________________.
2. ____________________.
3. ____________________.

3 Look at the pictures. Then complete the conversation.

LESSON 2

4 Write an occupation for each event.

1. a concert: *a singer*
2. a movie: ________
3. a game: ________
4. a dinner: ________

5 When is your English class? Circle the day or days. Write the times.

Monday	Tuesday	Wednesday	Thursday	Friday	Saturday	Sunday

6 What events are in your city or town this week? Complete the chart.

Name	Event	Day	Time	Place
Hee-Young Lim	*Concert*	*Saturday*	*7:00 P.M.*	*Music Center*

7 Look at the posters.

Now check true or false.

	true	false
1. The game is on Sunday.	☐	☐
2. The movie is at 7:10 on Wednesday.	☐	☐
3. The dinner is at half past seven.	☐	☐
4. The concert is at three o'clock.	☐	☐
5. The movie is at 3:40 on Saturday.	☐	☐

8 Look at the posters in Exercise 7 again. Complete the questions and answers.

1. A: ______________________________? B: It's _____ one o'clock.
2. A: ______________________________? B: It's _____ Friday _____ a quarter to eight.
3. A: ______________________________? B: It's _____ Thursday.
4. A: ______________________________? B: It's _____ Sunday _____ 3:00.

9 Complete the conversation. Use the times and days on the posters in Exercise 7.

1. **You:** Hi, ____________. How are you?

   Your friend: Fine, thanks. And you?

2. **You:** ____________. Look. There's a ____________ on ____________.

   Your friend: Great! What time?

3. **You:** ____________.

   Your friend: OK. Let's meet at ____________.

LESSON 3

10 **Match the ordinal numbers with the people. Draw lines.**

fifth first ninth eleventh seventh thirteenth

second twelfth sixth eighth fourth fifteenth

11 **Look at the pictures. Write the months for each type of weather where you live.**

1. ______________________________
2. ______________________________
3. ______________________________

12 **Complete the sentences with an ordinal number or a month.**

1. October is the ____________ month of the year.
2. ____________ is the fifth month of the year.
3. ____________ is the second month of the year.
4. March is the ____________ month of the year.
5. December is the ____________ month of the year.
6. ____________ is the eleventh month of the year.
7. June is the ____________ month of the year.
8. ____________ is the eighth month of the year.

13 Complete the conversations. Use the prepositions in, on, and at.

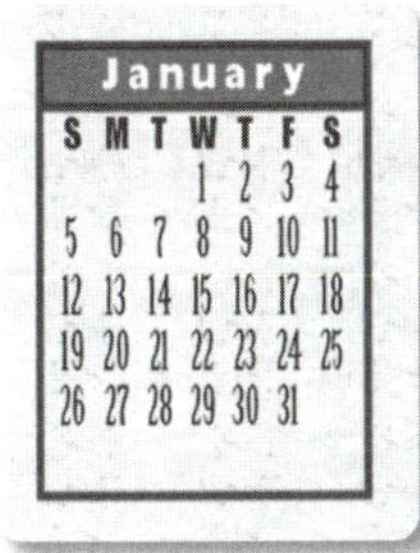

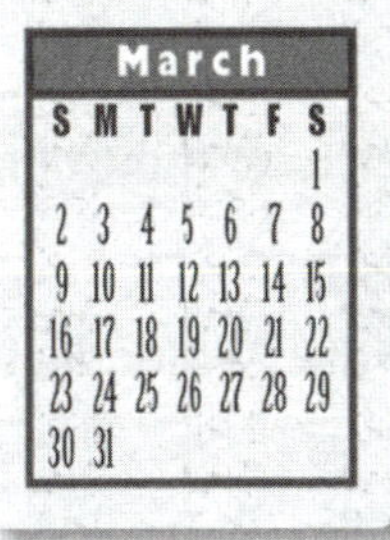

1. A: When's your birthday? B: It's ________ March. It's ________ March 11th.
2. A: Am I late? B: No, you're ________ time.
3. A: What time is the party? B: It's ________ 1:30.
4. A: Is the game at 9:15 tonight? B: No, it's ________ the afternoon, ________ 3:45.
5. A: When's the dance? B: ________ Saturday, ________ 8:00.
6. A: What time's the movie? B: It's ________ midnight.
7. A: Is the dinner in January? B: Yes, it's ________ the 19th.
8. A: There's a concert at 10:00. B: ________ night or ________ the morning?

14 Look at the invitation.

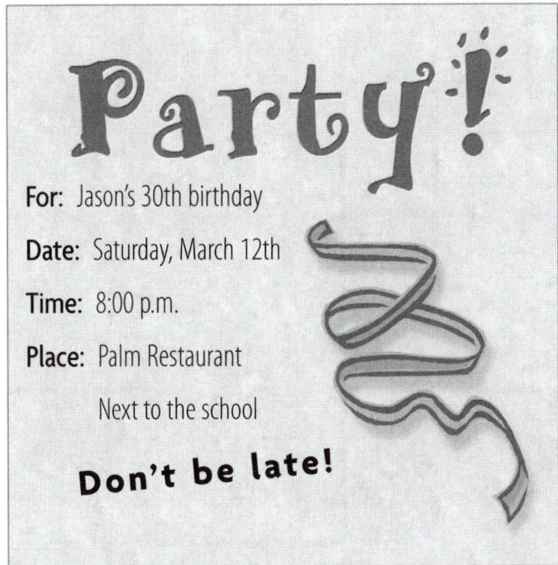
Party!

For: Jason's 30th birthday

Date: Saturday, March 12th

Time: 8:00 p.m.

Place: Palm Restaurant
Next to the school

Don't be late!

Now answer the questions. Write complete sentences.

1. What month is the party? It's in March.
2. What date is the party? ________________.
3. What day is the party? ________________.
4. What time's the party? ________________.
5. Where's the restaurant? ________________.

Fill in the answers. Then look at the numbers under the lines. Write the letters in the puzzle.

1. A dinner, a dance, or a concert ___ ___   ___ ___ ___ ___ ___ (12, 3, 10, 1)
2. The class is on weekdays—Mondays, Wednesdays, and ____. ___ ___ ___ ___ ___ ___ ___ (8, 4, 5, 11, 6)
3. An event with athletes ___   ___ ___ ___ ___ (13, 7)
4. April is the ____ month of the year. ___ ___ ___ ___ ___ ___ (9, 2)

Puzzle

"___ ___ ___ ___ ___   ___ ___   ___ ___ ___ ___   ___ ___ ___   ___ ___ ___ ___ ___ ___ ___ ___ ___ ___."

1 2 3 4 3   5 6   1 5 7 3   8 9 4   3 10 3 4 11 1 2 5 12 13

—Thomas Edison, inventor (U.S.)

Complete the puzzle.

Across

5. This month has twenty-eight days.
7. Jana's birthday is March 12th. What's her sign?
9. The movie's at 10:15. It's a quarter to ten now. You're ____.
10. Good ____! (at 7:00 P.M.)
13. Good ____! (at 7:00 A.M.)

Down

1. The ninth month of the year
2. The fourth weekday
3. The first day of the weekend
4. The time in New Delhi when it's noon in New York
6. Q is the ____ letter in the alphabet.
8. The baseball ____ is on Friday.
11. 12:00 A.M.
12. 12:00 P.M.

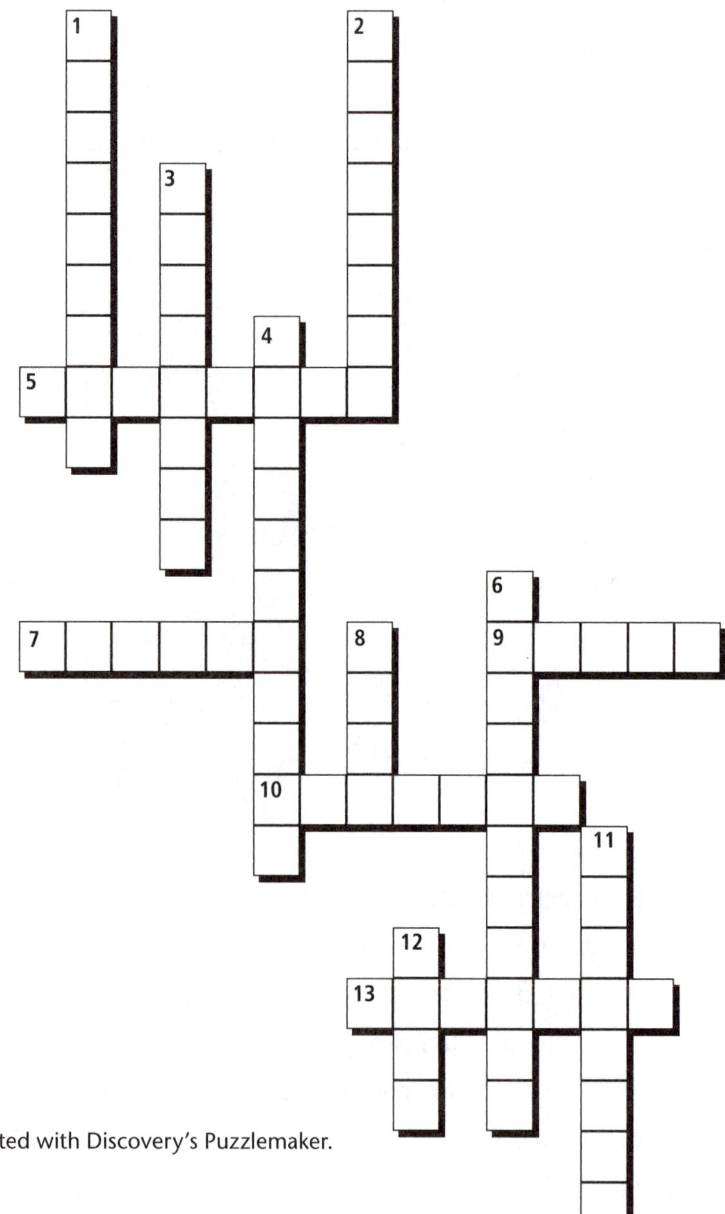

SOURCE: Created with Discovery's Puzzlemaker.

UNIT 6

Clothes

LESSON 1

Write the names of the clothes.

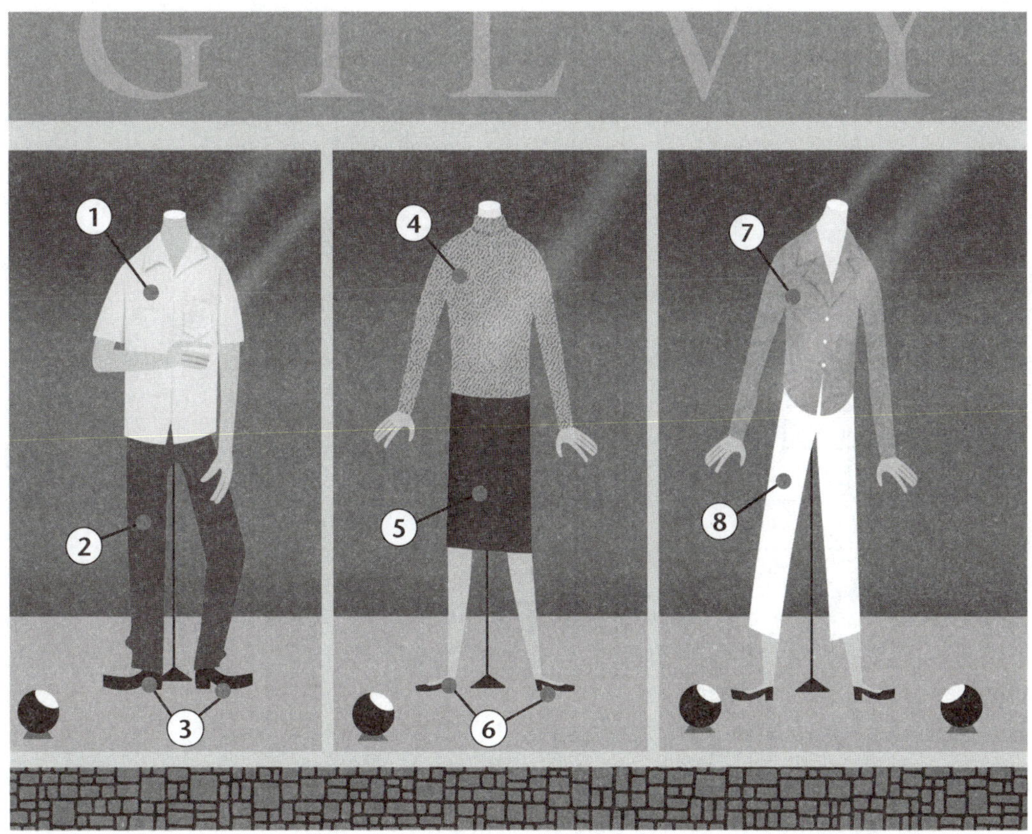

1. ______________________
2. ______________________
3. ______________________
4. ______________________
5. ______________________
6. ______________________
7. ______________________
8. ______________________

2 **Circle one of the clothing items in each picture. Write a sentence with I like and this, that, these or those.**

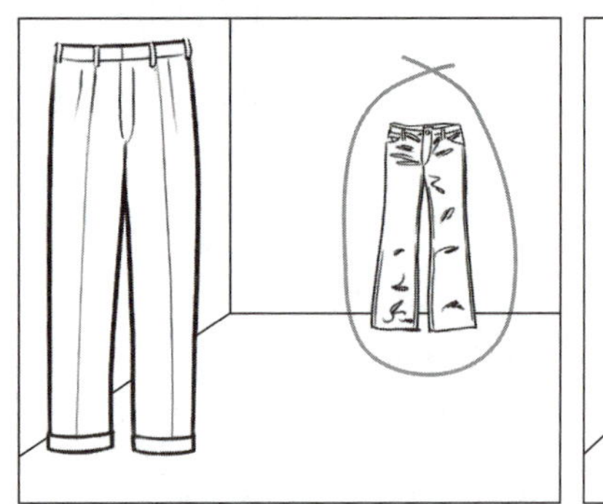

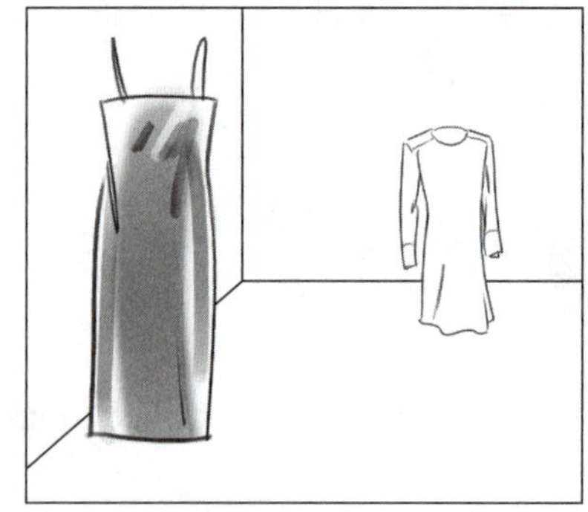

Example: I like those pants. 1. ______________________________ 2. ______________________________

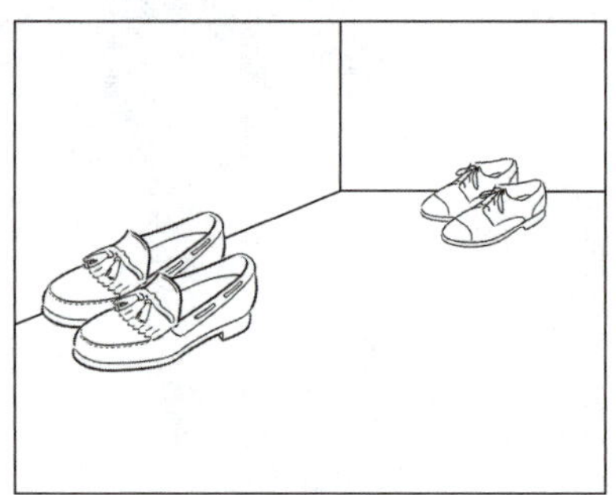

3. ______________________________ 4. ______________________________

3 **Write sentences. Use words from each list.**

I My sister / brother My parents My classmates My neighbor My friends My friend and I My teacher	+	like likes	+	restaurants bookstores weekends motorcycles parties dances movies concerts

1. My friends like parties.
2. ______________________________.
3. ______________________________.
4. ______________________________.
5. ______________________________.

4 **Look at the pictures. Complete the sentences. Use <u>want</u>, <u>need</u>, or <u>have</u>.**

1. They have a daughter.

2. ________________ a jacket.

3. ________________ that car.

4. ________________ a taxi.

5. ________________ a moped.

6. ________________ that tie.

5 **Look at the pictures. Compliment each person on his or her clothes.**

1. ____________________________________

____

____

2. ____________________________________

____

____

① 

② 

LESSON 2

6 Complete the sentences about yourself. Use like or don't like.

Example: I don't like ______ red jackets.

1. ______ brown suits.
2. ______ purple pants.
3. ______ black sweaters.
4. ______ white shoes.
5. ______ blue shirts / blouses.

7 Complete the sentences. Write the simple present tense of the verb.

1. My daughters ______ (want) those dresses.
2. Susan's friend ______ (not like) her skirt.
3. Michael and Steven ______ (not have) suits.
4. ______ you ______ (have) a jacket?
5. We ______ (need) shoes for the party.
6. ______ Anthony ______ (want) this tie?
7. ______ Ryan ______ (need) large or extra large?
8. They ______ (not have) this blouse in white.

8 Look at the clothes. Write a question. Ask for the color or size in parentheses. Then complete the short answer.

①

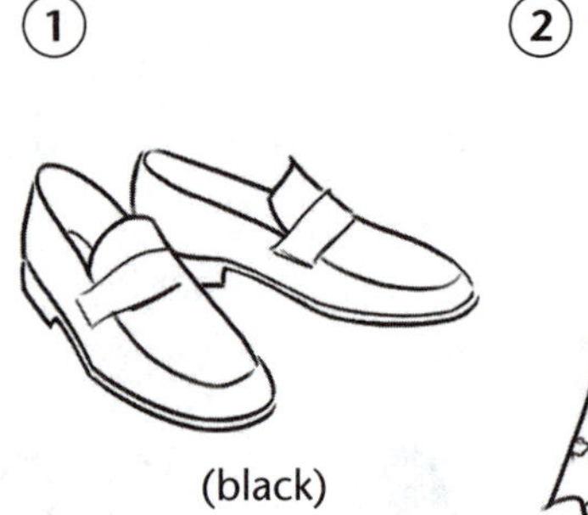

(black)

②

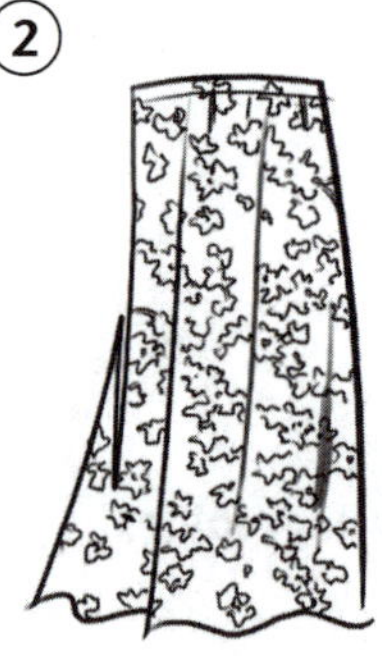

(small)

③

(brown)

④

(large)

1. Do you have these shoes in black ______? No, we don't ______.
2. ______? Yes, ______.
3. ______? Yes, ______.
4. ______? No, ______.

LESSON 3

9 Write sentences about yourself. Use <u>have</u> / <u>don't have</u>, <u>want</u> / <u>don't want</u>, or <u>need</u> / <u>don't need</u>.

Example: expensive shoes: I don't need expensive shoes.

1. a gray suit: ______.
2. new pants: ______.
3. a red sweater: ______.
4. a white shirt / blouse: ______.
5. a long jacket: ______.

10 Read about Elena and Marina.

Elena and Marina are looking for new clothes. They're at Fashionistas, a new clothes store. They need clothes for work. Elena is a manager, and Marina is a musician. Elena's suit is old, and she needs a new one. She wants new shoes, too. Marina needs a black dress for a concert on Saturday.

Fashionistas has a black suit, a gray suit, a brown suit, and a red suit in Elena's size. She likes the gray suit. Fashionistas has a short dress and a long dress in black. Marina wants the short dress. The long dress is very expensive. Fashionistas doesn't have shoes. Elena says, "Look! There's a shoe store across the street."

Now read the answers. Then write questions. Use <u>Why</u>, <u>What</u>, or <u>Which</u>.

1. A: ______? B: Because her suit is old.
2. A: ______? B: A suit and shoes.
3. A: ______? B: A black dress.
4. A: ______? B: The gray suit.
5. A: ______? B: The short dress.

11 Plan your clothes for next week. Write on the calendar.

Monday	Tuesday	Wednesday	Thursday	Friday	Saturday	Sunday
gray pants black sweater new black shoes						

12 Look at the pictures. Complete the questions and the answers.

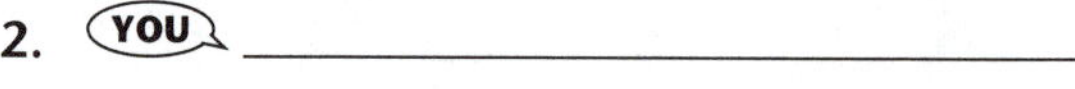

1. YOU ______________________________

______________________________.

2. YOU ______________________________

______________________________.

3. YOU ______________________________

______________________________.

4. YOU ______________________________

______________________________.

JUST FOR **FUN**

1 TAKE A GUESS! **Match the numbers with the letters to make these colors.**

1. _____ green
2. _____ orange
3. _____ purple
4. _____ brown
5. _____ gray

a. red and green
b. yellow and blue
c. yellow and red
d. black and white
e. blue and red

2 WORD FIND. **Look across (→) and down (↓). Circle the ten clothes and the ten colors. Then write the clothes and colors on the lines.**

I P U I K E K T S I R E I B Y C
J T S S S E K B R O W N R E L R
A U K W L W T T G U R B L E I D
C K I E L H E E U U R E G P G O
K W R A E I G R E L E A R A R K
E T T T K T C T T R A R E L A A
T I U E E E W O O A B L U E Y L
H E I R Y E L L O W N Y I D E H
G G R E E N R R N Y E L S R D O
T R E D P N K E S E O S S B R R
B G R E U E K I E E R H U R E U
L A S G R N O B A R A I I I S W
A U H A P I G S L R N R T L S T
C W O L L P A N T S G T B O I S
K R E O E K E A H A E B U T R Y
N H L R R H H R I B L O U S E E

Source: Created with spellbuilders.com.

Clothes

Colors

Guess: 1. b; 2. c; 3. e; 4. a; 5. d

UNIT 7

Activities

LESSON 1

1 YOUR MORNING ACTIVITIES. **Put the activities in order. Write ordinal numbers (1st, 2nd, . . .) on the lines. Write an X next to the activities you don't do.**

_____ take a shower / bath

_____ eat breakfast

_____ put on makeup

_____ get up

_____ shave

_____ get dressed

_____ brush my teeth

_____ comb / brush my hair

Choose your first three morning activities. What time do you do them?

Example: I get up at 7:00.

1. ______________________________.
2. ______________________________.
3. ______________________________.

2 **Look at the activities and the times. Write sentences in the simple present tense.**

1. She comes home at 6:30.

2. ______________________________.

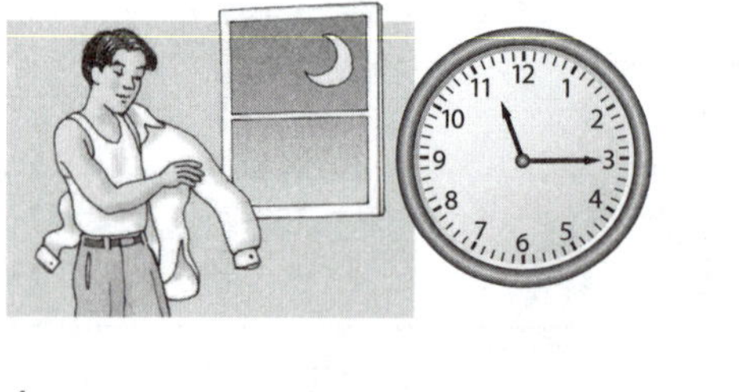

3. ______________________________.

4. ______________________________.

3 Write the name of a family member or friend. Check his or her activities.

Name: ____________________

- ☐ takes a shower in the evening
- ☐ takes a shower in the morning
- ☐ doesn't eat breakfast
- ☐ eats a large breakfast
- ☐ studies after dinner
- ☐ watches TV after dinner
- ☐ gets up early on weekends
- ☐ gets up late on the weekend

Now write sentences about this person.

4 Look at the responses. Write questions with When or What time.

1. A: When does Karina take a shower?
   B: Karina takes a shower in the morning.
2. A: ____________________?
   B: Robert goes to bed after midnight. He's an evening person.
3. A: ____________________?
   B: My children? They watch TV on weekends, in the morning.
4. A: ____________________?
   B: I study after dinner.
5. A: ____________________?
   B: Julia gets up at 5:00 A.M. on weekdays.
6. A: ____________________?
   B: They come home early—before 5:00 P.M.

5 Complete the conversation.

Are you a morning person or an evening person?

1. YOU ____________________.

And why do you say that?

2. YOU ____________________.

LESSON 2

6 **On a typical weekday, do you . . . ? Check always, usually, sometimes, or never.**

	always	usually	sometimes	never
1. eat breakfast	☐	☐	☐	☐
2. watch TV in the evening	☐	☐	☐	☐
3. take a shower at night	☐	☐	☐	☐
4. read after 10:00 P.M.	☐	☐	☐	☐
5. exercise in the morning	☐	☐	☐	☐
6. take a nap in the afternoon	☐	☐	☐	☐
7. go out for lunch	☐	☐	☐	☐

On a typical weekend, do you . . . ? Check always, usually, sometimes, or never.

	always	usually	sometimes	never
1. visit friends	☐	☐	☐	☐
2. go dancing	☐	☐	☐	☐
3. study	☐	☐	☐	☐
4. go to the movies	☐	☐	☐	☐
5. play soccer	☐	☐	☐	☐
6. check e-mail	☐	☐	☐	☐
7. go out for dinner	☐	☐	☐	☐

7 **Look at your answers in Exercise 6. Write five sentences about your activities. Follow the model.**

Example: On weekdays, I usually exercise in the morning.

1. ______________________________.
2. ______________________________.
3. ______________________________.
4. ______________________________.
5. ______________________________.

8 **Think about the leisure activities of family members and friends. Complete the chart.**

Name / Relationship	Activity	Time expression	Frequency
grandfather	take a nap	in the afternoon	usually

Now write sentences about the leisure activities of family members and friends. Use your chart.

Example: My grandfather usually takes a nap in the afternoon.

1. ______________________________.
2. ______________________________.
3. ______________________________.
4. ______________________________.
5. ______________________________.

LESSON 3

9 **Look at Larry's weekly schedule.**

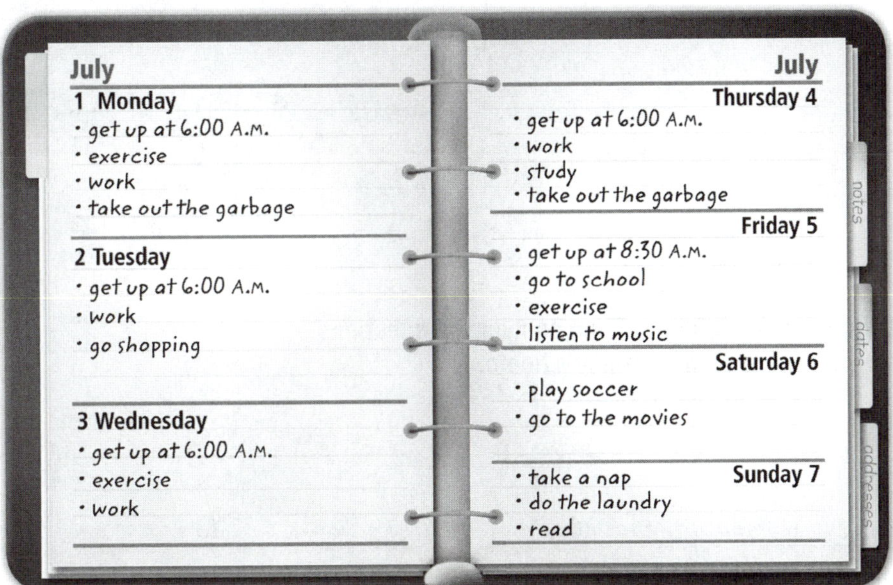

July
1 Monday
• get up at 6:00 A.M.
• exercise
• work
• take out the garbage
2 Tuesday
• get up at 6:00 A.M.
• work
• go shopping
3 Wednesday
• get up at 6:00 A.M.
• exercise
• work
July
Thursday 4
• get up at 6:00 A.M.
• work
• study
• take out the garbage
Friday 5
• get up at 8:30 A.M.
• go to school
• exercise
• listen to music
Saturday 6
• play soccer
• go to the movies
Sunday 7
• take a nap
• do the laundry
• read
notes
dates
addresses

Now write questions with How often and complete the answers.

1. A: How often does Larry go to school?

   B: He ______________ once a week.

2. A: ______________________________?

   B: He ______________ twice a week.

3. A: ______________________________?

   B: He ______________ three times a week.

4. A: ______________________________?

   B: He ______________ four times a week.

10 **Look at Larry's schedule in exercise 9 again. Answer the questions.**

1. When does Larry work? ______________________________.
2. When does he go to school? ______________________________.
3. What's his typical day like? ______________________________.
4. What time does he get up on Fridays? ______________________________.
5. What does he do in his free time? ______________________________.

11 **Look at the pictures. Then write sentences about the household chores Mr. and Mrs. Rand do.**

Mr. Rand

1. ______________________________.
2. ______________________________.

Mrs. Rand

3. ______________________________.
4. ______________________________.
5. ______________________________.

12 **Write a question with <u>Who</u> for each picture. Then answer the questions with information about your home or your family's home.**

Example: Who does the laundry ______________? I do ______.

1. ______________________________? ______________.
2. ______________________________? ______________.
3. ______________________________? ______________.
4. ______________________________? ______________.

JUST FOR **FUN**

1 A RIDDLE FOR YOU!

What comes once in an afternoon, twice in a week, but never in a day or month?

(Hint: It comes once in the alphabet.)

Answer: ____________________

2 WORD FIND. Look across (→) and down (↓). Circle the fourteen activities. Then write the activities in the correct column.

W	A	T	C	H	T	V	U	C	E	A	K	A	U	H	I	T
E	P	N	A	C	O	H	C	L	H	S	O	I	K	V	R	I
K	L	W	A	S	H	T	H	E	D	I	S	H	E	S	E	A
G	A	L	M	S	G	A	N	A	M	C	T	M	N	M	A	M
E	Y	L	M	G	O	A	L	N	K	B	A	O	H	A	D	K
T	S	O	R	O	D	T	N	T	S	D	K	W	W	K	W	O
V	O	A	G	T	A	A	T	H	A	A	E	T	N	E	V	O
A	C	E	D	O	N	S	C	E	U	N	A	H	I	D	A	I
C	C	S	A	W	C	Y	H	H	O	M	B	E	A	I	W	I
U	E	N	U	O	I	C	S	O	E	U	A	L	O	N	H	E
U	R	S	R	R	N	B	T	U	T	E	T	A	D	N	S	E
M	L	N	S	K	G	E	G	S	O	O	H	W	A	E	A	E
C	H	C	B	D	O	T	H	E	L	A	U	N	D	R	Y	D
T	E	L	I	S	T	E	N	T	O	M	U	S	I	C	H	D
T	E	T	A	K	E	A	N	A	P	E	N	H	A	O	I	E
L	H	T	I	A	K	N	T	T	U	E	W	W	N	S	S	A

Source: Created with ed.helper.com.

Chores / Work activities	**Leisure activities**
____________________	____________________
____________________	____________________
____________________	____________________
____________________	____________________
____________________	____________________
____________________	____________________
____________________	____________________

Riddle: the letter e

UNITS 1–7

Review

1 Circle the word or phrase that is different.

1. athlete	classmate	neighbor	colleague
2. doctor	engineer	pharmacy	scientist
3. last name	weekend	address	phone number
4. subway	moped	train	game
5. brother	daughter	wife	grandmother
6. tall	new	handsome	young
7. concert	party	restaurant	movie
8. skirt	blouse	dress	tie
9. listen to music	do the laundry	visit friends	go to the movies
10. get up	shave	come home	eat breakfast

2 Read the ad for an event.

Women's Soccer
Russia and Brazil
The Sports Center
Saturday, May 15th
1:00 P.M.
Tickets on sale now!
www.sportstix.com

Now write a question for each answer.

1. **A:** ____________________?
   B: A soccer game.
2. **A:** ____________________?
   B: The Sports Center.
3. **A:** ____________________?
   B: At one o'clock.
4. **A:** ____________________?
   B: On Saturday, May 15th.

3 Read about Salma Hayek.

This is Salma Hayek. She's an actor. She's from Mexico, but her name is Arabic. Her father's family is from Lebanon. Her mother is Mexican. Her father is a businessman, and her mother is an opera singer. She has one brother, Sami Hayek. Salma Hayek's birthday is September 2, 1966. She's a Virgo. She is short and very pretty. In September 2007, Hayek became a mother. She and her husband have a daughter. Her name is Valentina Paloma.

Salma Hayek's 2002 movie *Frida* is not very old, but it's already a classic. It is the winner of two Academy Awards—for music and for makeup. The movie is about the famous Mexican artist Frida Kahlo. Hayek is Frida in the movie. Alfred Molina is her husband, the artist Diego Rivera. Many of Hayek's friends are in the movie. The acting is great. The colors, art, clothes, and music in *Frida* are beautiful.

Source: Adapted from www.imdb.com

Now answer the questions.

1. What does Salma Hayek do? ______________________.
2. Is she from Lebanon? ______________________.
3. Does Hayek have brothers and sisters? ______________________.
4. When is her birthday? ______________________.
5. How old is she? ______________________.
6. Is she tall? ______________________.
7. How old is her daughter? ______________________.
8. What is her daughter's first name? ______________________.

4 Compare Frida Kahlo and Salma Hayek. Complete the chart. Use the reading in Exercise 3.

	Frida Kahlo	Salma Hayek
Occupation	artist	
Nationality	from Mexico	
Nationality of father	from Germany	
Nationality of mother	from Mexico	
Brothers and sisters	3 sisters, no brothers	
Birthday	July 6, 1907	

5 **Choose one family member, friend, neighbor, or colleague. Complete the information.**

1. Name: ______
2. Relationship to you: ______
3. Occupation: ______
4. Birthday, age (how old?), sign: ______
5. Adjectives to describe the person: ______
6. Leisure activities: ______

Now write about this person. Use the information above.

OPTIONAL VOCABULARY BOOSTER ACTIVITIES

Look at the pictures. Write a <u>yes</u> / <u>no</u> question with <u>be</u> and a short answer. Use the words in parentheses.

1. 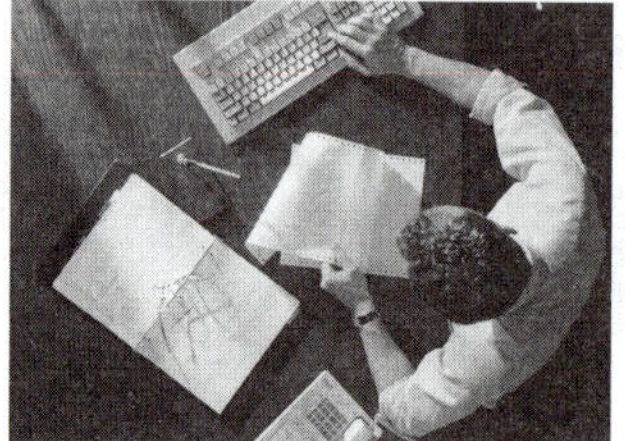

A: Is he a bank teller?
(bank teller)
B: No, he's not.

2. 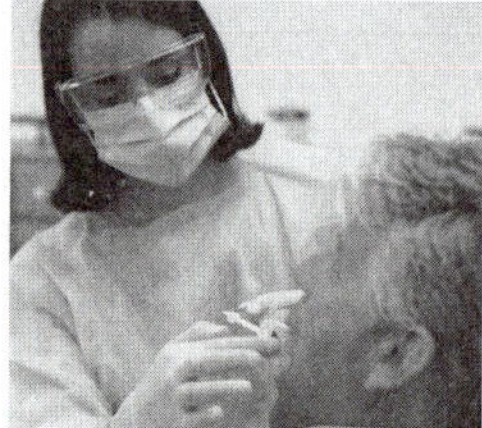

A: ______?
(doctor)
B: ______.

3. 

A: ______?
(lawyer)
B: ______.

4. 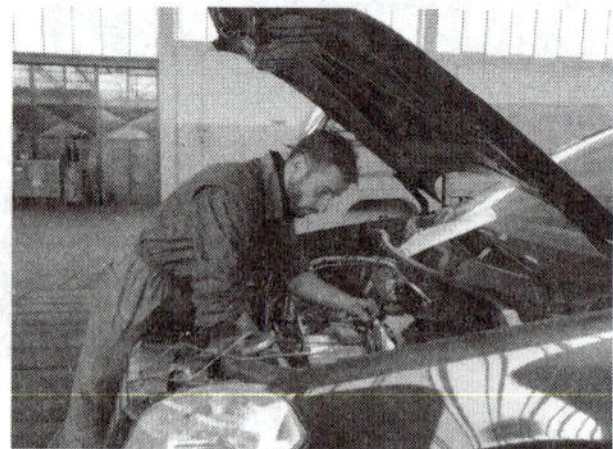

A: ______?
(electrician)
B: ______.

5.

A: ______?
(florist)
B: ______.

6. 

A: ______?
(hairdresser)
B: ______.

2 Look at the pictures. Write answers to the questions. Remember to capitalize proper nouns.

1. What is the grocery clerk's name? His name is Sam.
2. What is the pharmacist's name? ______________________.
3. What is the waiter's name? ______________________.
4. What is the travel agent's first name? ______________________.
5. What is the professor's last name? ______________________.

3 Answer a friend's questions about your neighborhood.

1. How do you go to the supermarket? ______________________
2. Can I walk to the dry cleaners? ______________________
3. Where's the video store? ______________________

4 Which events do you like? Number the events from 1 to 8 in the order you like them.

_____ plays

_____ ballets

_____ operas

_____ speeches

_____ art exhibitions

_____ baseball games

_____ volleyball games

_____ football games

5 Write this, that, these, or those and the names of the clothes.

Do you like ________________________?
1.

I need ________________________, but I
2.
want ________________________.
3.

Are ________________________
4.
black or blue?

Look at ________________________.
5.
They're really nice.

6 Look at the pictures. Ask for a different color or size. Write yes / no questions with have.

1. *Do you have these sandals in red*________________________?

2. ____?

3. ____?

4. ____?

5. ____?

7 Look at the pictures and the answers. Write the questions.

1. A: How often do you dust?

   B: Twice a month.

2. A: ______________ you ______________?

   B: On Sundays.

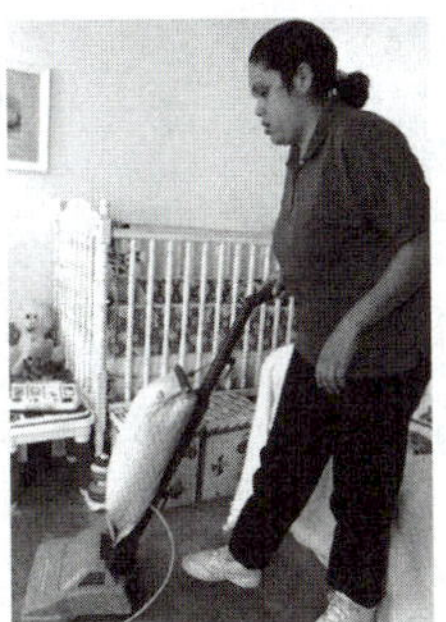

3. A: ______________________________?

   B: My wife does.

4. A: ______________________________?

   B: Yes, I do.

UNIT 8

Home and Neighborhood

LESSON 1

1 **Complete the conversations. Use prepositions of place and the verb be or the simple present tense.**

1. A: Where ______________ you ______________?
   B: We live ______________ an apartment.
2. A: ______________ your building have an elevator?
   B: No, but it's OK. I live ______________ the first floor.
3. A: ______________ you a student?
   B: Yes, I study ______________ the English School.
4. A: ______________ you ______________ near the school?
   B: Yes. I live ______________Third Avenue.
5. A: Where ______________ you ______________?
   B: I work ______________ an office. I'm a manager.
6. A: Where ______________ your son work?
   B: He ______________ ______________ Center Restaurant. He's a chef.
7. A: ______________ he ______________ near the restaurant?
   B: No, he lives ______________ Bank Street.

2 **Look at the pictures of places in New York City. What is the place? Write a sentence.**

Metropolitan Museum of Art

Central Park

Grand Central Terminal

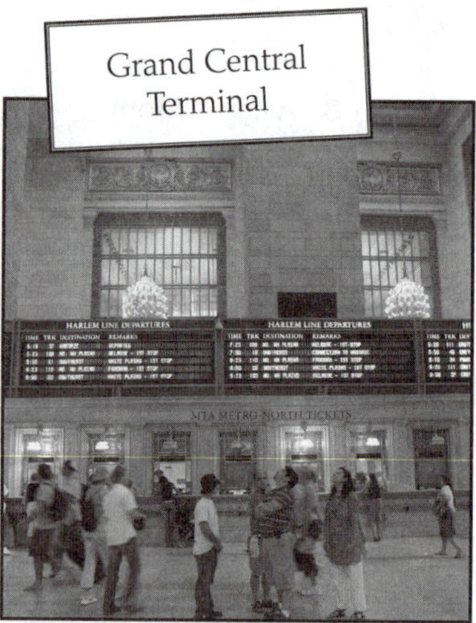

1. It's a museum. 2. ______________. 3. ______________.

John F. Kennedy International Airport

Russian Tea Room

Yankee Stadium

4. ______________________. 5. ______________________. 6. ______________________.

3 Complete the charts.

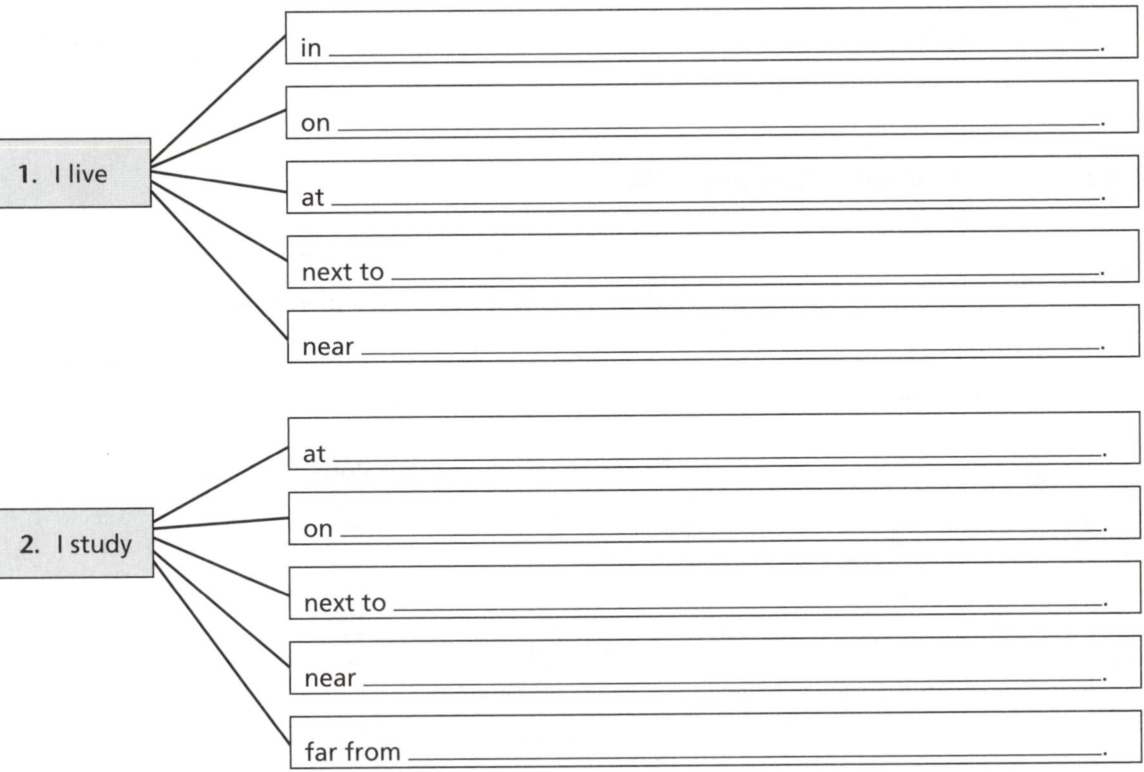

1. I live
in ______________________.
on ______________________.
at ______________________.
next to ______________________.
near ______________________.
2. I study
at ______________________.
on ______________________.
next to ______________________.
near ______________________.
far from ______________________.

4 Answer the questions with real information.

Example: Is the airport far from your school? Yes. About 45 minutes by bus.

1. Is the mall far from your school? ______________________.
2. Is the bus station far from your school? ______________________.
3. Is the hospital far from your school? ______________________.

LESSON 2

5 Look at the floor plans for two apartments. What are they like? Write sentences with There's and There are.

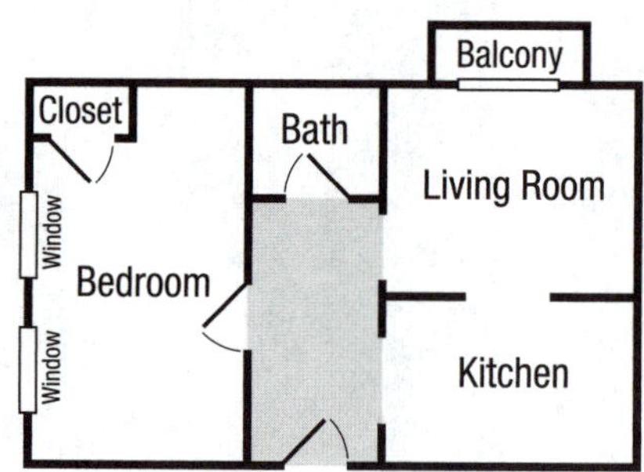

1. There's one large bedroom ____________.
2. ____________.
3. ____________.
4. ____________.
5. ____________.
6. There are three bedrooms ____________.
7. ____________.
8. ____________.
9. ____________.
10. ____________.

6 Complete the information about your home.

1 Circle one:

house

apartment

2 Check ✔ the rooms in your home.

☐ kitchen
☐ living room
☐ dining room
☐ bedroom(s)

3 How many do you have in your home?

bathroom(s) ____ bedroom(s) ____ closet(s) ____

4 Check ✔ yes or no. Does your home have . . .

	yes	no
a garden?	☐	☐
a garage?	☐	☐
a balcony?	☐	☐
a large kitchen?	☐	☐
a second floor?	☐	☐
a large closet?	☐	☐

7 **Add your city to the list. Describe your home and the home of someone you know.**

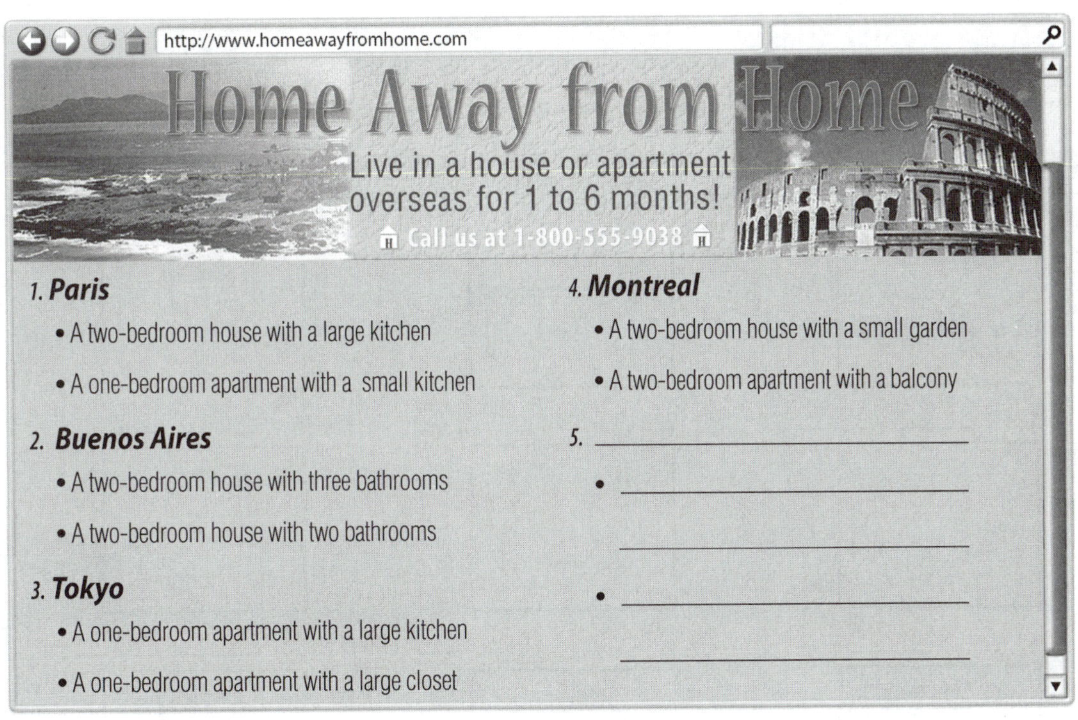

1. **Paris**
   - A two-bedroom house with a large kitchen
   - A one-bedroom apartment with a small kitchen
2. **Buenos Aires**
   - A two-bedroom house with three bathrooms
   - A two-bedroom house with two bathrooms
3. **Tokyo**
   - A one-bedroom apartment with a large kitchen
   - A one-bedroom apartment with a large closet
4. **Montreal**
   - A two-bedroom house with a small garden
   - A two-bedroom apartment with a balcony
5. ____________________
   - ____________________
     ____
   - ____________________
     ____

8 **Look at Exercise 7 again. Circle the house or apartment you like. Describe the home. Write complete sentences.**

Example: *It's a house. It's in Paris. There are two bedrooms...*

____

____

____

Now write two questions to ask about the house or apartment. Use Is there, Are there, or How many.

1. ______________________________?
2. ______________________________

LESSON 3

9 **What new furniture or appliances do you want for your home? Make a list of four items that you want.**

Example: *a new sofa for the living room*

1. ______________________________
2. ______________________________
3. ______________________________
4. ______________________________

10 **Label the furniture on the website.**

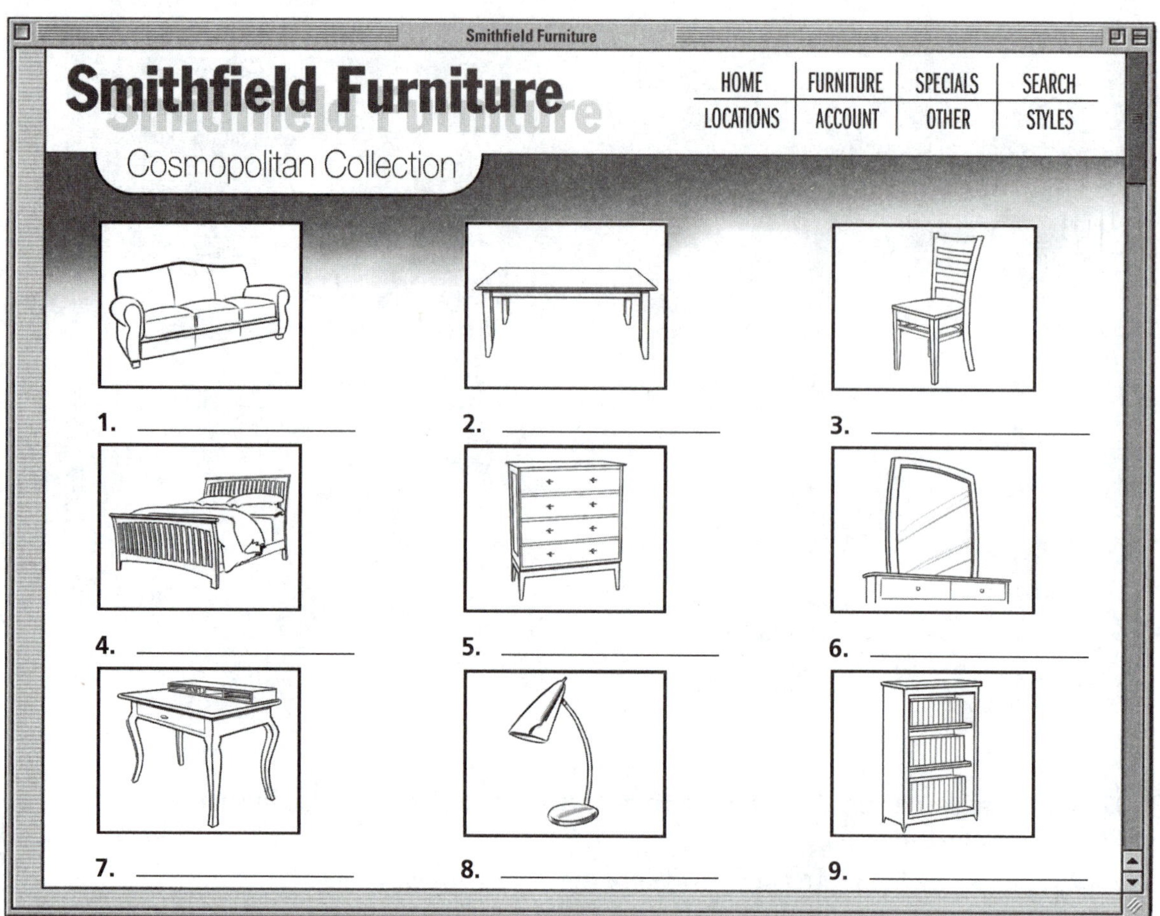

11 **Complete the conversation. Give your opinion about the furniture in Exercise 10.**

1. "This is a great desk. What do you think?"
   YOU ____.
2. "I like this bookcase, too. What about you?"
   YOU ____.
3. "Look at this lamp. Do you think it's nice?"
   YOU ____.
4. "What do you think of this chair?"
   YOU ____.

12 **Describe one room in your home.**

JUST FOR **FUN**

A RIDDLE FOR YOU! Read the clues. Look at the map. Then write the names of the rooms in Paul and Paula's apartment.

- The living room is between their bedroom and the dining room.
- The bathroom is near the living room. It's right across the hall.
- The kitchen is next to the bathroom, on the left.
- Their daughter's bedroom is near their bedroom. It's right across the hall.
- The dining room is not the first room.

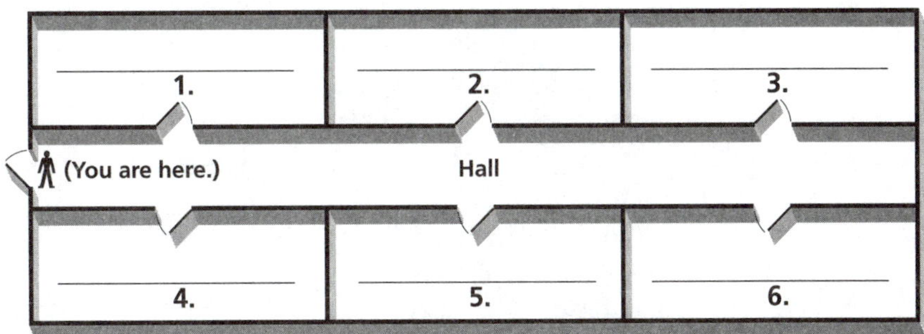

2 **Complete the puzzle.**

Across

1. The room where the shower is
3. A place to see famous artists' work
4. Don't take the elevator. The _____ is good exercise.
5. The office is on the thirty-second floor. Take the _____.
9. Joe lives in an apartment. His _____ has four floors.
11. A place for your clothes
12. A bed, a sofa, and a desk are all _____.
13. A refrigerator, a stove, and a TV are all _____.
14. A place to go shopping

Down

2. A place where doctors and nurses work
6. This is a nice table. What do you _____?
7. The room where the fridge is
8. Not beautiful
10. Very pretty

Source: Created with Discovery's Puzzlemaker.

Riddle: 1. kitchen; 2. bathroom; 3. daughter's bedroom; 4. dining room; 5. living room; 6. bedroom

UNIT 9 Activities and Plans

LESSON 1

1 **How's the weather? Is it hot, cold, warm, or cool?**

1. ______________________.

2. ______________________.

3. ______________________.

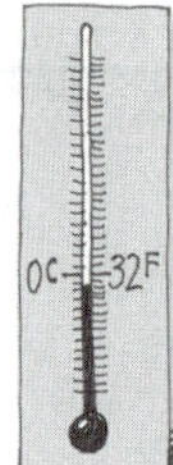

4. ______________________.

2 **Look at the pictures. What are the people doing right now? Write sentences in the present continuous.**

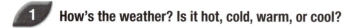

1. She's brushing her teeth.

2. ______________________.

3. ______________________.

4. ______________________.

5. ______________________.

6. ______________________.

3 **Look at the pictures. Answer the questions. Use a short answer and the present continuous.**

1. Is he taking a bath?
   No, he isn't. He's taking a shower.

2. Is she reading?
   ______________________________________.

3. Are they listening to music?
   ______________________________________.

4. Is she wearing a dress?
   ______________________________________.

5. Is it snowing?
   ______________________________________.

4 **Where's Andrea? What's she doing? Match the rooms with Andrea's activities.**

1. _____ She's in the kitchen.
2. _____ She's in the bedroom.
3. _____ She's in the bathroom.
4. _____ She's in the dining room.
5. _____ She's in the office.
6. _____ She's in the living room.

a. She's going to bed.
b. She's checking e-mail.
c. She's eating dinner with her family.
d. She's reading on the sofa.
e. She's brushing her teeth.
f. She's making breakfast.

5 **Look at the Ryan family's living room. Then read the answers and write questions about the family's activities. Use the present continuous.**

1. *Where's the grandfather taking a nap* ? On the sofa.
2. ______________________________ ? Washing the dishes.
3. ______________________________ ? They're going to a concert.
4. ______________________________ ? The son is.
5. ______________________________ ? An apple.
6. ______________________________ ? She's playing in the chair.

6 **Imagine a very nice day. Answer the questions in complete sentences.**

1. Where are you? ______________________________.
2. Who's with you? ______________________________.
3. What are you doing? ______________________________.
4. How's the weather? ______________________________.
5. What are you wearing? ______________________________.

7 **Write the present participles.**

1. take ____________
2. play ____________
3. study ____________
4. exercise ____________
5. eat ____________
6. do ____________
7. drive ____________
8. call ____________
9. go ____________
10. get dressed ____________

LESSON 3

8 Write the time, date, month, or year.

1. right now: ______________
2. today: ______________
3. tomorrow: ______________
4. the day after tomorrow: ______________
5. this month: ______________
6. this year: ______________

9 Answer the questions in the present continuous.

1. What are you doing today? ______________________________.
2. What are you doing tonight? ______________________________.
3. What are you doing tomorrow? ______________________________.
4. What are you doing tomorrow evening? ______________________________.
5. What are you doing this weekend? ______________________________.

10 Respond to the instant messages with your own information. Create your own screen name.

Message

chatsalot21: Hi. I'm in Los Angeles. I'm working here this week. Where are you?

__________: ______________________________

chatsalot21: What are you doing?

__________: ______________________________

chatsalot21: How's the weather there?

__________: ______________________________

chatsalot21: The weather is beautiful here! It's warm and sunny. Hey, are you doing anything special this weekend?

__________: ______________________________

chatsalot21: I'm playing soccer on Saturday morning. Do you want to get together on Saturday afternoon?

__________: ______________________________

11 Write your plans for next week. Write sentences in the present continuous.

JUST FOR
FUN

First, unscramble the letters of the time expressions. Then write the correct letters in the numbered boxes to complete the puzzle.

Time expressions

1. GITHR ONW 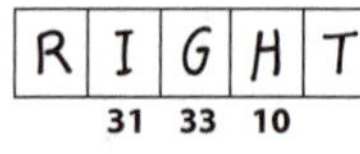

31 33 10 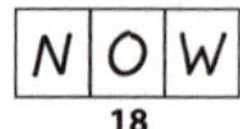

18

2. YOADT 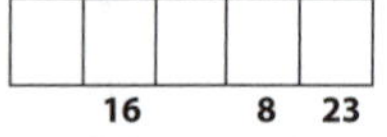
16 8 23

3. NTTOHGI 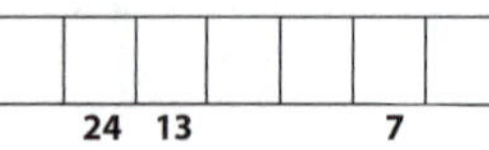
24 13 7

4. TISH NMRINGO 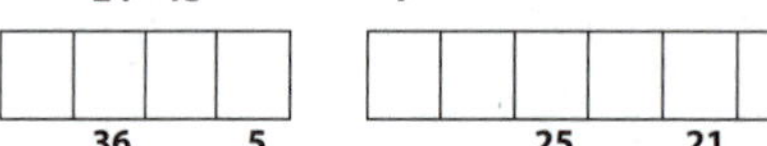
36 5 25 21

5. TSHI NATRONFEO 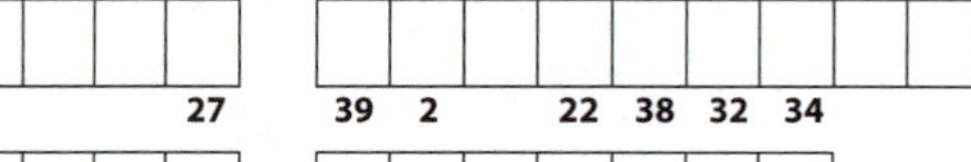
27 39 2 22 38 32 34

6. HITS GENNIVE 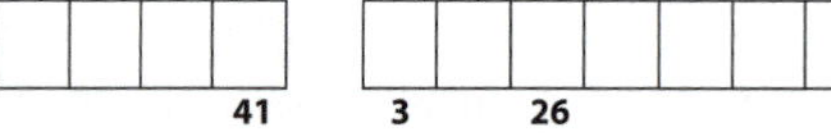
41 3 26

7. OMTORWOR 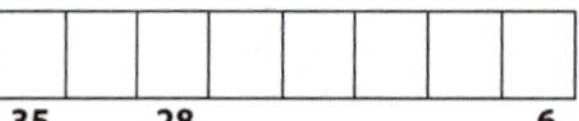
35 28 6

8. TEH YDA TFREA TOOWORRM 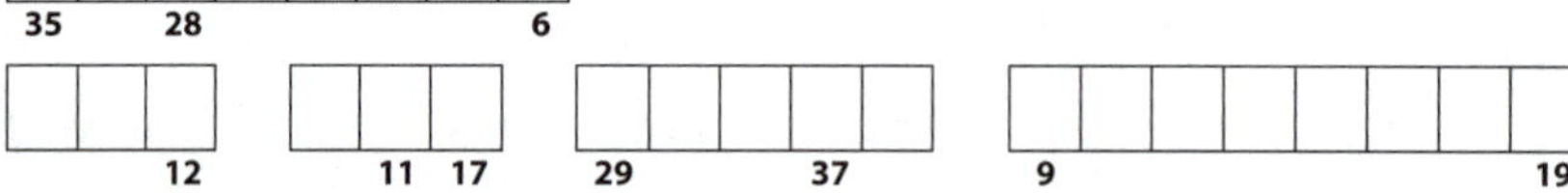
12 11 17 29 37 9 19

9. STIH EEKW
15 1 30

10. TISH MOTHN
4 14 40 20

Puzzle

" 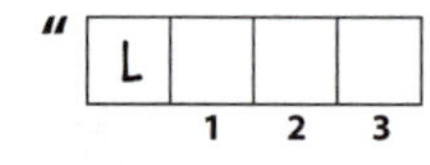

1 2 3 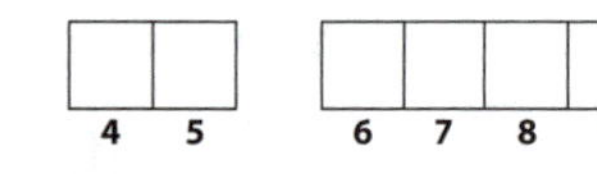
4 5 6 7 8 9 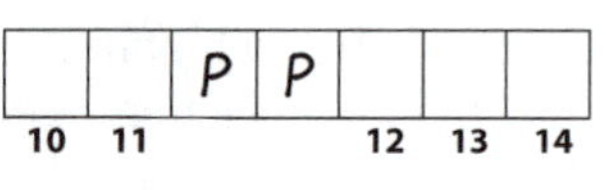

10 11 12 13 14 15 16 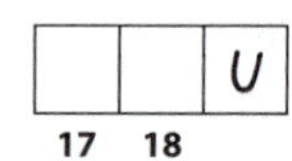

17 18

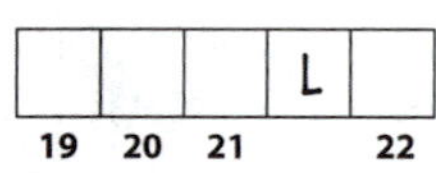

19 20 21 22 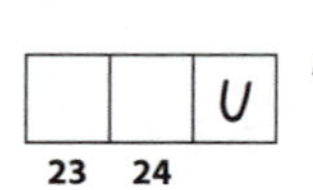

23 24 ' 25 26 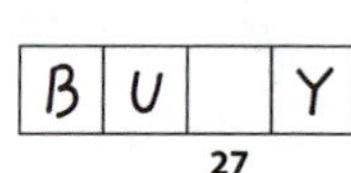

27 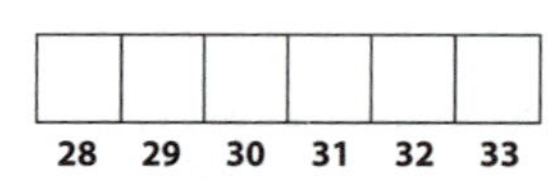
28 29 30 31 32 33

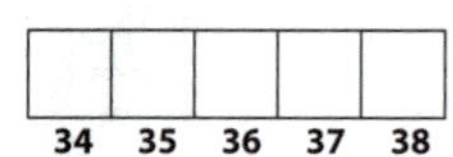
34 35 36 37 38 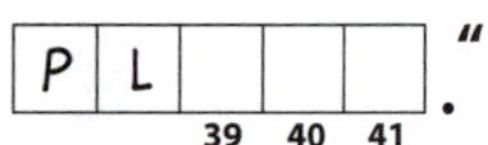

39 40 41 ."

—John Lennon, singer and musician (U.K.)

Source: Created with Discovery's Puzzlemaker.

2 **TAKE A GUESS!** **Match the weather and the places.**

1. _____ Number 1 hot place in the world	a. Plateau Station, Antarctica
2. _____ Number 1 cold place in the world	b. Eastern Sahara Desert, Africa
3. _____ Number 1 rainy place in the world	c. Ben Nevis, Scotland
4. _____ Number 1 snowy place in the world	d. Mount Baker, Washington, U.S.A.
5. _____ Number 1 sunny place in the world	e. Cherrapunji, India
6. _____ Number 1 cloudy place in the world	f. Dallol, Ethiopia

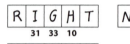

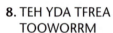

Take a Guess: 1. f; 2. a; 3. e; 4. d; 5. b; 6. c

UNIT 10

Food

LESSON 1

1 Complete the chart. Check the boxes.

	oranges	bananas	eggs	tomatoes	apples	lemons	peas	peppers	potatoes	beans	onions
I like											
I don't like											
I have in my kitchen											
I need											
I eat every day											
I sometimes eat											
I never eat											

2 Look at the recipe.

Ingredients:
3 potatoes
6 eggs
1 small tomato
1/2 an onion
1/2 a pepper

Now answer the questions.

1. Are there any potatoes in the omelet? ______________________.
2. How many eggs are there in the omelet? ______________________.
3. Are there any onions? ______________________.
4. How many tomatoes are there in the omelet? ______________________.
5. Which ingredients do you have for this recipe? ______________________.
6. Which ingredients do you need? ______________________.

3 Write questions with How many. Then answer the questions.

1. students / your English class: How many students are there in your English class?
   ______________________________.
2. people / your family: ______________________________?
   ______________________________.
3. days / this month: ______________________________?
   ______________________________.
4. sweaters / your closet: ______________________________?
   ______________________________.
5. bathrooms / your home: ______________________________?
   ______________________________.

LESSON 2

4 Count or non-count? Write a, an, or X before each food or drink.

1.	_____ tea	5.	_____ egg	9.	_____ cheese
2.	_____ rice	6.	_____ sugar	10.	_____ lemon
3.	_____ banana	7.	_____ oil	11.	_____ juice
4.	_____ meat	8.	_____ apple	12.	_____ onion

5 Do you keep these foods in the fridge? On the shelf? On the counter? Write four sentences.

I keep soup, pasta, and sugar on the shelf.

juice	bread	milk
rice	butter	eggs
oil	tomatoes	tea

1. ______________________________.
2. ______________________________.
3. ______________________________.
4. ______________________________.

6 What color is it? What color are they? Write sentences.

1. milk: Milk is white.
2. eggs: ______________________________.
3. butter: ______________________________.
4. orange juice: ______________________________.
5. tomatoes: ______________________________.
6. coffee: ______________________________.

7 Label the pictures.

1. a loaf of bread

2. ______

3. ______

4. ______

5. ______

8 Write five sentences. Use words or phrases from each box.

How many How much Is there any Are there any	+	meat juice oranges sugar bananas onions bread cans of soup	+	in the fridge? are there on the counter? do we have? is there? on the shelf? do you want? are there? in the kitchen?

1. Are there any oranges in the fridge?
2. ______
3. ______
4. ______
5. ______
6. ______

9 Look at the picture.

Complete the questions with <u>How much</u> or <u>How many</u>. Then answer the questions.

1. A: ____________ peppers are there? B: ____________.
2. A: ____________ water is in the fridge? B: ____________.
3. A: ____________ bags of beans are there? B: ____________.
4. A: ____________ soda is there? B: ____________.

10 Look at the picture in Exercise 9 again. Complete the questions with <u>Are there any</u> or <u>Is there any</u>. Then answer the questions.

1. A: ____________ cheese in the fridge? B: ____________.
2. A: ____________ eggs? B: ____________.
3. A: ____________ juice? B: ____________.
4. A: ____________ butter? B: ____________.

11 What do you want for dinner? Answer the questions in a restaurant.

1. "Would you like tomato soup or onion soup?"
   YOU ____________.
2. "Would you like chicken or meat?"
   YOU ____________.
3. "Would you like potatoes or brown rice?"
   YOU ____________.
4. "Would you like coffee or tea later?"
   YOU ____________.
5. "And then would you like an apple or an orange?"
   YOU ____________.

LESSON 3

12 Complete each sentence. Circle the letter.

1. Robert _____ his e-mail every day.
   a. check b. checks c. is checking
2. Theresa _____ the laundry on Mondays.
   a. do b. does c. is doing
3. Lucas and Nate aren't at home. They _____ soccer in the park.
   a. play b. plays c. are playing
4. I _____ chicken with peppers for dinner. Would you like to join me?
   a. make b. makes c. am making
5. Mr. and Mrs. Juster usually _____ meat.
   a. doesn't eat b. don't eat c. aren't eating

13 Complete the conversations. Use the simple present tense or the present continuous.

1. A: What ________________ (you / eat) right now?
   B: Chicken soup.
2. A: ________________ (he / want) milk in his coffee?
   B: No, he doesn't. But he would like sugar.
3. A: What ________________ (we / have) in the fridge?
   B: Soda, cheese, and an apple.
4. A: I ________________ (wear) a dress to the party. How about you?
   B: I never ________________ (wear) dresses.
5. A: ________________ (Jeff / work) on Saturdays?
   B: Yes, usually. But this Saturday he ________________ (play) soccer.
6. A: Where ________________ (you / eat) lunch on Tuesdays?
   B: At Eli's Café. But today we ________________ (go) to City Bistro for my boss's birthday.

JUST FOR **FUN**

1 A RIDDLE FOR YOU!

George, Helen, and Steve are drinking coffee. Bart, Karen, and Dave are drinking soda. Is Ellie drinking coffee or soda?

(Hint: Look at the letters in each drink.)

Answer: ______________

Source: able2know.com

2 Complete the puzzle.

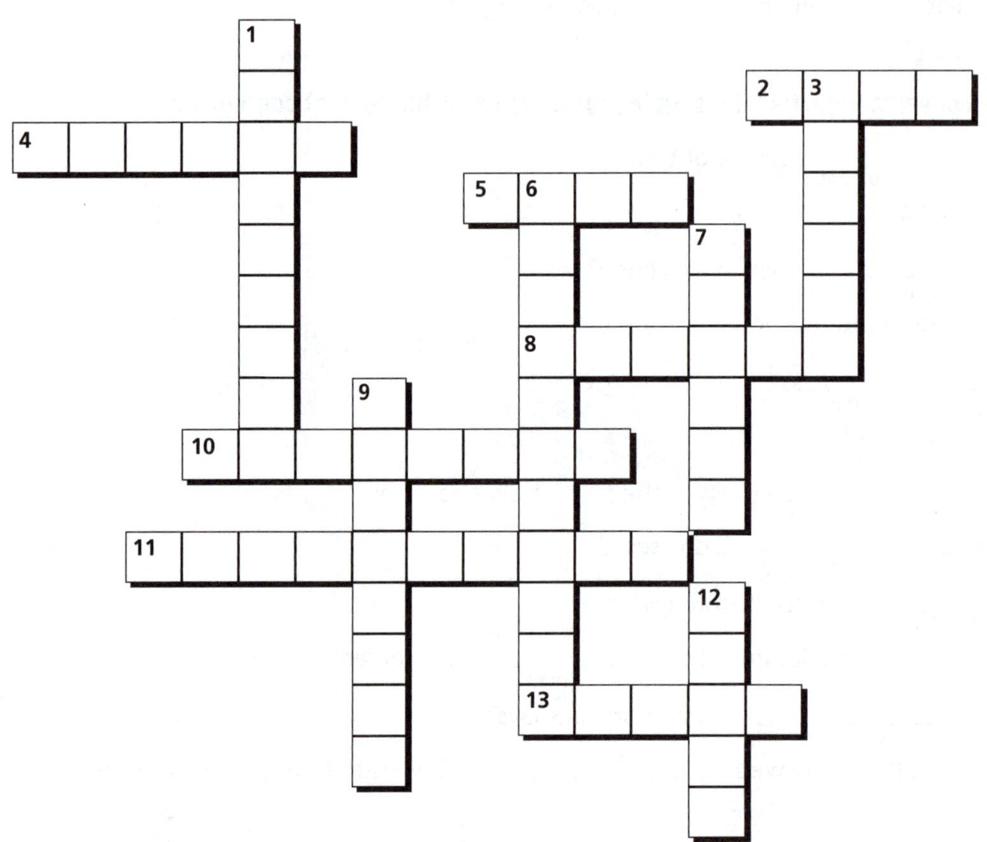

Across

2. A _____ of bread
4. Salt and _____.
5. In Asia, people eat a lot of _____.
8. Directions for cooking something
10. You make this drink with lemons, water, and sugar.
11. A box, a bottle, a bag, and a can are all _____.
13. I like coffee with milk and _____.

Down

1. The place for milk: _____ _____
3. Would you like apple juice, _____ juice, or tomato juice?
6. The foods in a recipe
7. Water, tea, and soda are all _____.
9. In the omelet, there are three _____.
12. Peppers, peas, and _____ are green.

Source: Created with Discovery's Puzzlemaker.

Riddle: Ellie is drinking coffee.

UNIT 11

Past Events

LESSON 1

1 **Write the date, month, or year.**

1. yesterday: ____________________
2. last Wednesday: ____________________
3. three days ago: ____________________
4. one week ago: ____________________
5. the day before yesterday: ____________________
6. last month: ____________________
7. two months ago: ____________________
8. last year: ____________________
9. five years ago: ____________________

2 **Complete the questions with <u>was</u> or <u>were</u>. Then answer the questions.**

1. Where *were* you last night at 9:00? *I was at home*.
2. ________ you at school yesterday? ____________________.
3. How ________ the weather last week? ____________________.
4. ________ there milk in your refrigerator this morning? ____________________.
5. What ________ your first e-mail address? ____________________.
6. When ________ your birthday? ____________________.
7. How old ________ you in 2005? ____________________.
8. Who ________ a famous person from the twentieth century? ____________________.

3 **Look at the list of events from <u>last week</u>.**

Special Events at The Hill School

Monday: Afternoon Concert
Tuesday: Teachers' Dinner
Wednesday: Volleyball Game: Teachers vs. Students
Thursday: Breakfast for Students
Friday: Movie
Saturday: Movie (afternoon) / Dance (evening)
Sunday: Exercise Classes

All events are free.
Check the school's website for places and times.

Now write sentences about the events. Use <u>There was</u> or <u>There were</u>.

1. ____________________.
2. ____________________.
3. ____________________.
4. ____________________.

LESSON 2

4 **Complete the paragraph. Use the simple past tense forms of the verbs in the box. Use each verb only once.**

be	eat	put	buy
come	get	see	not exercise
drive	go	take	not read

Amy __________ (1) home late last night. She and her colleagues __________ (2) a movie after work. After the movie, they __________ (3) out for dinner. This morning Amy __________ (4) up at 8:00. She usually gets up at 7:00. She __________ (5) a shower and got dressed by 8:15. She usually takes the bus to work, but today she __________ (6). In the car, she __________ (7) on her makeup and __________ (8) a banana for breakfast. She __________ (9), and she __________ (10) the newspaper. But Amy __________ (11) only five minutes late to work! Later, she __________ (12) a cup of coffee at a restaurant near her office building.

5 **Write five sentences about your activities this morning. Look at the pictures for ideas.**

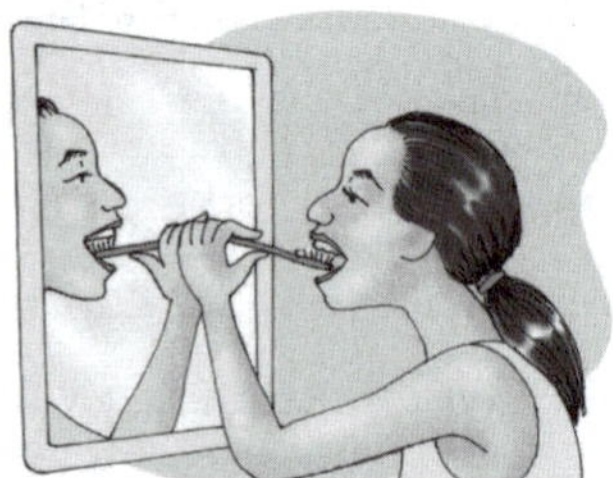

6 Read the status updates. Ask a question. Use the simple past tense.

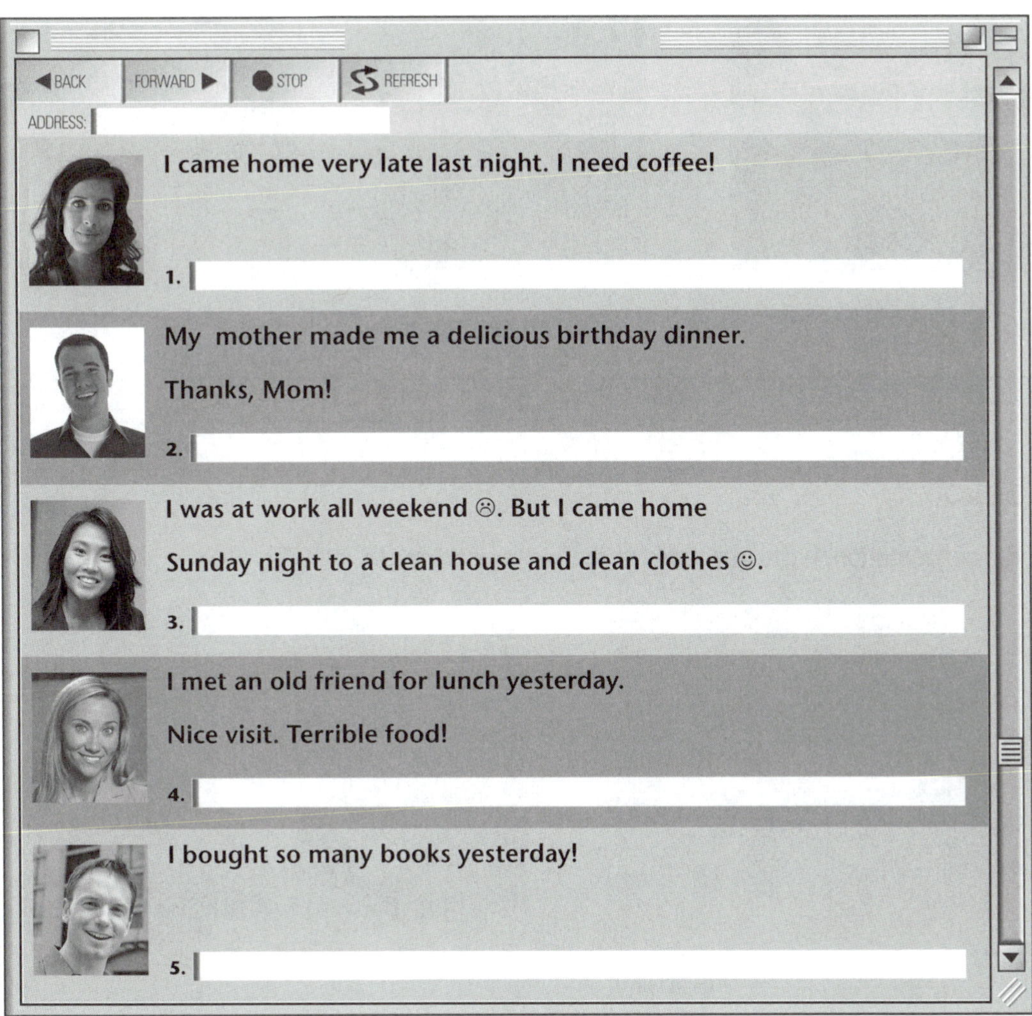

BACK
FORWARD
STOP
REFRESH
ADDRESS:
I came home very late last night. I need coffee!
1.
My mother made me a delicious birthday dinner.
Thanks, Mom!
2.
I was at work all weekend ☹. But I came home
Sunday night to a clean house and clean clothes ☺.
3.
I met an old friend for lunch yesterday.
Nice visit. Terrible food!
4.
I bought so many books yesterday!
5.

LESSON 3

7 Which activities do you like? Number the activities from 1 to 6 in the order you like to do them.

_____ go to the beach
_____ go swimming
_____ go for a walk
_____ go running
_____ go bike riding
_____ go for a drive

Which activities did you do? Which activities didn't you do? Write three sentences about yesterday, last week, and two weeks ago.

Examples: I went to the beach yesterday.

I didn't go bike riding last week.

1. ______________________________.
2. ______________________________.
3. ______________________________.

8 Write three things you did last weekend. Write three things you didn't do.

What I did:

1. ______________________________
2. ______________________________
3. ______________________________

What I didn't do:

1. ______________________________
2. ______________________________
3. ______________________________

9 Complete the conversation. Write questions in the simple past tense.

1. A: ______________________________?
   B: Actually, I had a great weekend.
2. A: ______________________________?
   B: I went to the beach.
3. A: ______________________________?
   B: It was sunny and warm.
4. A: ______________________________?
   B: Some friends from school.
5. A: ______________________________?
   B: We went swimming and bike riding.

10 Choose the correct responses to complete the conversation. Write the letter on the line.

1. A: Hi. How's it going?
   B: _____
2. A: Friday night? Let me think . . . Oh, yeah, I went shopping. Why?
   B: _____
3. A: There was? Too bad I wasn't there!
   B: _____
4. A: Well, I exercised, I did the laundry, and then I studied.
   B: _____
5. A: Actually, I had a great day on Sunday. The weather was beautiful, so I went bike riding at the beach.
   B: _____

a. There was a great concert at the stadium.
b. So what did you do on Saturday?
c. Not bad. Hey, where were you on Friday night?
d. Now that sounds nice!
e. What about Sunday? Did you do anything special on Sunday?

11 Answer the questions. Use the simple past tense.

1. Who did you talk to first today? ________________________.
2. What did you do the day before yesterday? ________________________.
3. What time did you come home last Saturday night? ________________________.
4. Did you do anything special last weekend? ________________________.
5. Did you have a good day yesterday? ________________________.
6. How many books did you read last month? ________________________.
7. Where did you live five years ago? ________________________.
8. How often did you watch TV last week? ________________________.

JUST FOR
FUN

1 A RIDDLE FOR YOU!

Where is the only place that yesterday always comes after today?

(Hint: Think of a book.)

Answer: ____________________

Source: didyouknow.cd.

2 WORD FIND. Look across (→) and down (↓). Circle the base forms of 21 verbs. Then write the simple past tense forms of those verbs on the lines.

T H I N K C U T E T G
T A K E S E E C A W E
T C O M E C C A T S T
T E L I K E T U E A I
H N C E H A V E V Y Y
V U T D R I V E O C A
S T U D Y E D R I N K
W R I T E M A K E A T
E S C L E A N P L A Y
E X E R C I S E B U Y
W A T C H R E A D L A

Source: Created at armoredpenguin.com.

Riddle: In a dictionary

UNIT 12

Appearance and Health

LESSON 1

1 Check the adjectives that describe you.

1. My hair

☐ black	☐ blonde	☐ straight	☐ short
☐ brown	☐ gray	☐ wavy	☐ long
☐ red	☐ white	☐ curly	☐ bald

2. My eyes

☐ brown	☐ blue	☐ green

2 Describe a family member, a friend, or a colleague. Fill in the chart.

	Hair			
Person	Color	Straight, wavy, or curly	Long, short, or bald	Eye color
My brother	blonde	straight	short	blue

3 Write the parts of the face.

eyebrow	nose
eye	mouth
eyelashes	chin
ear	hair

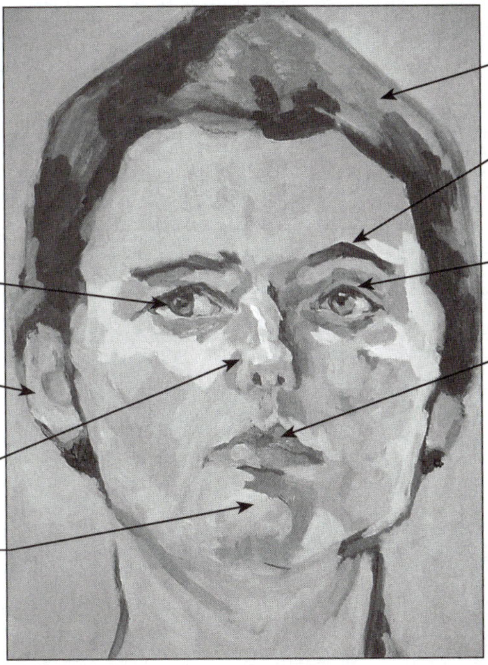

1. ____________
2. ____________
3. ____________
4. ____________
5. ____________
6. ____________
7. ____________
8. ____________

4 **Look at Exercise 1 again. Use the information to write sentences with <u>be</u> about yourself.**

Example: My hair is brown ______.

1. ______.
2. ______.
3. ______.

5 **Look at Exercise 2 again. Use the information to write sentences with <u>have</u> about a family member, a friend, or a colleague.**

Example: My brother has blue eyes ______.

1. ______.
2. ______.
3. ______.

6 **Choose three famous people to describe.**

Here's language you already know:

pretty	short
handsome	tall
good-looking	old
cute	young

1. Johnny Depp: He's handsome. He has long, wavy, brown hair. His eyes are brown. He's an actor from the United States.
2. ______: ______
3. ______: ______
4. ______: ______

LESSON 2

hand	arm	neck
head	foot	leg
shoulder	knee	stomach
hip	chest	ankle

7 **Write the parts of the body. Use words from the box.**

1. ____________________
2. ____________________
3. ____________________
4. ____________________
5. ____________________
6. ____________________
7. ____________________
8. ____________________
9. ____________________
10. ____________________
11. ____________________
12. ____________________

8 **What happened? Write a sentence about each picture.**

1. *She burned her hand* ____________________.
2. ____________________.
3. ____________________.
4. ____________________.
5. ____________________.

Now complete the conversation.

6. A: ____________________?

   B: I hurt my arm.

7. A: ____________________?

   B: Actually, yes. It does.

LESSON 3

9 **Check the remedies for each ailment.**

	take something	lie down	have some tea	see a doctor	see a dentist	don't go to work or school	eat	don't eat
a cold								
a fever								
a sore throat								
a stomachache								
a backache								
a toothache								

10 **Think about an ailment you had. Then answer the questions.**

1. What was wrong? ______________________________.
2. What did you do? ______________________________.

Be careful!
Lie is irregular in the simple past tense:
lie (down) → lay (down)

11 **Your friend Brendan is going out with a colleague tonight. He wants your advice. Answer his questions.**

1. **Brendan:** "We're going to the movies. What should we see?"
   YOU ______________________________
2. **Brendan:** "After the movie, we're going out for dinner. Where should we go?"
   YOU ______________________________
3. **Brendan:** "Should I talk about work?"
   YOU ______________________________
4. **Brendan:** "What should I wear?"
   YOU ______________________________

JUST FOR
FUN

First, unscramble the letters of the ailments. Then write the correct letters in the numbered boxes to complete the puzzle.

Ailments

1. ONT ELEF LLEW  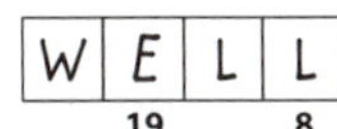

W E L L 19 8
2. A ODLC 4
3. A UOCHG 7
4. A RESO OTARHT 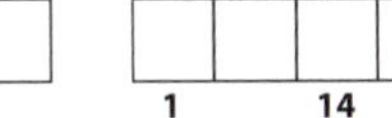 10 13
5. A SOACHHCAETM 15
6. A EEVFR 1 14
7. A AADEECHH  9 6
8. NA REAHEAC  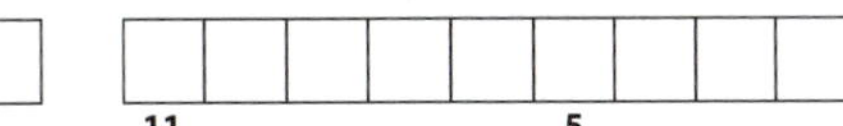 3 16
9. A KCABEACH  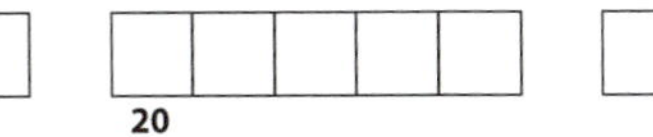 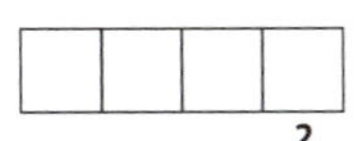 12 18
10. A OOTTHCHEA 11 5
11. A YNURN SEON 20 2

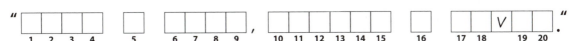

Puzzle

" 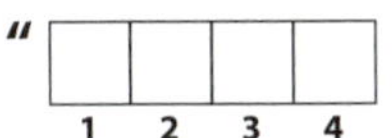  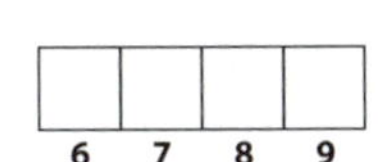, 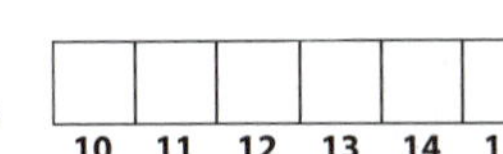 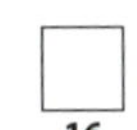 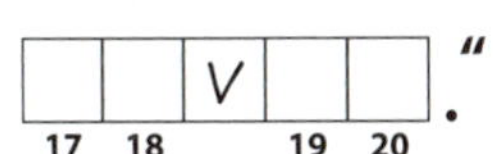."

—An old saying

2 Complete the puzzle.

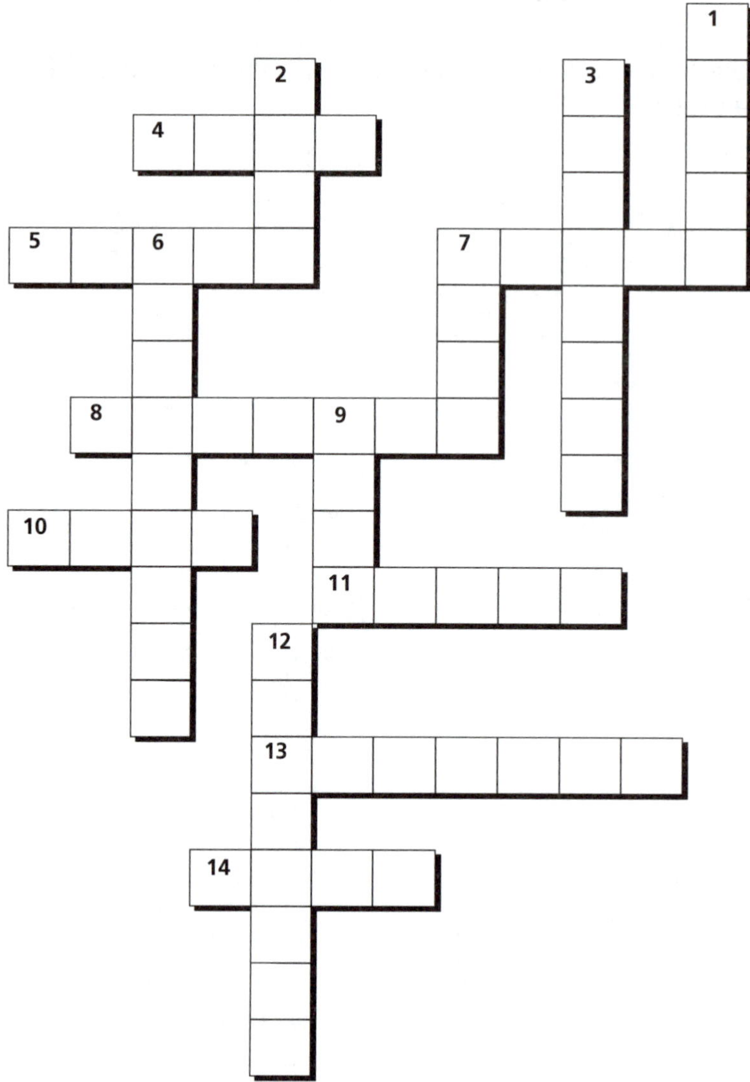

Across

4. It's between your hip and your ankle.

5. Hair on a man's chin

7. They're white. They're in your mouth.

8. They're on your hands. You have ten.

10. Parts of the body for shoes

11. Not long

13. It's between your hips and your chest.

14. Doesn't have hair

Down

1. It's between your nose and your chin.

2. Part of the body for a hat

3. Take something, lie down, and have some tea are all _____.

6. Burn your finger, cut your hand, and fall down are all _____.

7. They're on your feet. You have ten.

9. What you use to see

12. Hair between a man's nose and mouth

Source: Created with Discovery's Puzzlemaker.

UNIT 13

Abilities and Requests

LESSON 1

1 Write about four different people's abilities. Write sentences with well or badly.

Example: My sister: Rose knits well.

1. My teacher: ______.
2. My friend: ______.
3. My neighbor: ______.
4. My colleague: ______.

2 Look at the pictures. Write a sentence with can or can't.

1. She can play the guitar.
2. ______.
3. ______.
4. ______.

3 Complete the conversations with can or can't and the base form of a verb.

1. A: ______ you ______ English?
   B: Oh, yes, and I ______ ______ Spanish, too.
2. A: ______ you ______ my computer?
   B: No. I ______ fix cars but not computers.
3. A: ______ you ______?
   B: Yes, I can paint, but not very well.
4. A: ______ your sister ______?
   B: No. She ______ sew, but she ______ knit.
5. A: ______ your brothers ______ the violin?
   B: No, but they ______ ______ the guitar.

4 Which occupation is good for you? Take the *Top Notch* Abilities and Interests Survey.

Top Notch Abilities and Interests Survey

ABILITIES	Do very well	Do well	Do OK	Do badly	Can't do
1. paint	◯	◯	◯	◯	◯
2. draw	◯	◯	◯	◯	◯
3. dance	◯	◯	◯	◯	◯
4. swim	◯	◯	◯	◯	◯
5. drive	◯	◯	◯	◯	◯
6. play the violin	◯	◯	◯	◯	◯
7. ski	◯	◯	◯	◯	◯
8. fix a car	◯	◯	◯	◯	◯
9. cook	◯	◯	◯	◯	◯
10. sing	◯	◯	◯	◯	◯

INTERESTS	Like a lot	Like	Like a little	Don't like
1. go to concerts	◯	◯	◯	◯
2. go to museums	◯	◯	◯	◯
3. listen to music	◯	◯	◯	◯
4. make dinner for friends	◯	◯	◯	◯
5. exercise	◯	◯	◯	◯
6. go running	◯	◯	◯	◯
7. go bike riding	◯	◯	◯	◯
8. go for a drive	◯	◯	◯	◯

RESULTS

Look at your answers.
What do you do very well? What do you like to do a lot?

Can you cook well? Do you like to make dinner for friends?	Maybe you should be a chef.
Can you sing, dance, play the violin (guitar, piano, other instruments)? Do you like to go to concerts and listen to music?	Maybe you should be a singer or musician.
Can you swim and ski? Do you like to exercise and go running and bike riding?	Maybe you should be an athlete.
Can you draw and paint? Do you like to go to museums?	Maybe you should be an artist.
Can you drive and fix a car? Do you like to go for a drive?	Maybe you should be a mechanic.

According to the survey, what should you be? ________________________________

5 Describe your abilities. Complete the sentences.

1. I ________________ well, but I ________________ badly.
2. I can ________________ but not very well.
3. I can't ________________ at all.
4. I wish I could ________________.

LESSON 2

6 Write sentences with <u>too</u> and an adjective.

1. She can't drive.
   She's too young.

2. She can't watch TV.
   ________________.

3. You can't wear that shirt.
   ________________.

4. He doesn't want that suit.
   ________________.

5. We can't go bike riding today.
   ________________.

6. She can't drink this coffee.
   ________________.

7 Complete the sentences with adjectives from the box.

busy	tired	full	early	late	hungry

1. I went to a party last night. I got home at midnight and got up at 5:00 for work. I'm so ____________.
2. I'm really sorry, but I can't go to the movies now. It's ____________. I'm going home and going to bed.
3. That lunch was delicious! I had black bean soup, pasta with chicken, and bread. Now I'm ____________.
4. You get up at 5:30 every day for work? That's very ____________!
5. I don't want any dinner tonight. I had a late lunch today, and I'm not very ____________.
6. Today I have three meetings, lunch with my manager, a colleague's birthday party, and my son's soccer game. I'm very ____________.

8 Decline the invitations. Give reasons.

1. "Let's go for a drive."
   YOU ____.
2. "I'm going out for lunch. Would you like to join me?"
   YOU ____.
3. "How about a movie tonight? There's a show at 10:00."
   YOU ____.
4. "Let's go to the park."
   YOU ____.

LESSON 3

9 Match the problems with the requests. Write the letter on the line.

1. _____ I'm cold.
2. _____ I need to check my e-mail.
3. _____ It's too hot.
4. _____ I don't have any clean clothes.
5. _____ I can't read this.
6. _____ There isn't any milk.

a. Could you please do the laundry?
b. Could you please close the window?
c. Could you please turn on the computer?
d. Could you please go shopping?
e. Could you please open the window?
f. Could you please hand me my glasses?

10 Mrs. Cole's boss is coming for dinner at 6:00. But look at the house!

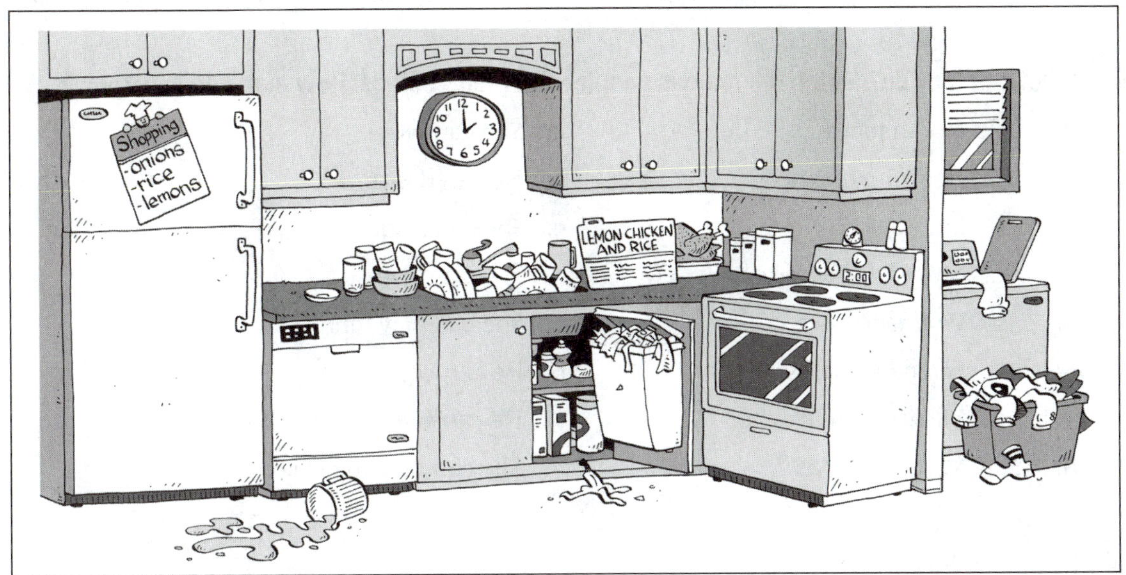

Help Mrs. Cole ask her husband to help. Write requests with could you.

1. Could you please take out the garbage ?
2. ______________________________?
3. ______________________________?
4. ______________________________?
5. ______________________________?

11 Choose the correct response. Circle the letter.

1. Can you sing?
   a. No. I sing very badly. b. I'm sorry, but I'm busy. c. No, thanks.
2. I wish I could ski. Can you?
   a. My pleasure. b. I'm too tired. c. Yes, I can.
3. Let's go out for dinner.
   a. I'm sorry to hear that. b. I'm sorry, but I'm busy. c. I'd like fish, please.
4. Could you do me a favor?
   a. Of course. b. That's too bad. c. Really?
5. Could you please turn off the TV?
   a. Sounds great. b. Sure. No problem. c. Maybe some other time.

JUST FOR **FUN**

1 What can they do? Match the famous people with their abilities. How many do you know?

1. _____ Norah Jones	a. She can write.
2. _____ Hee-Young Lim	b. He can dance.
3. _____ J.K. Rowling	c. She can sing.
4. _____ Mikhail Baryshnikov	d. He can drive.
5. _____ Wolfgang Puck	e. She can play tennis.
6. _____ Serena Williams	f. He can cook.
7. _____ Michael Schumacher	g. He can swim.
8. _____ Michael Phelps	h. She can play the cello.

2 Complete the puzzle.

Across

6. Play the guitar, swim, and drive are all _____.

9. A baby can do this at three months.

10. Make clothes

11. You can do this when there's snow.

12. I can't today. _____ some other time.

13. Not hungry

Down

1. Not well

2. These shoes are size 35. She needs a 37. They're _____ _____.

3. I'm cold. Could you please _____ my sweater?

4. Shakira can do this.

5. I'm going to bed. Could you please _____ the light?

7. Make dinner

8. You can do this at the beach.

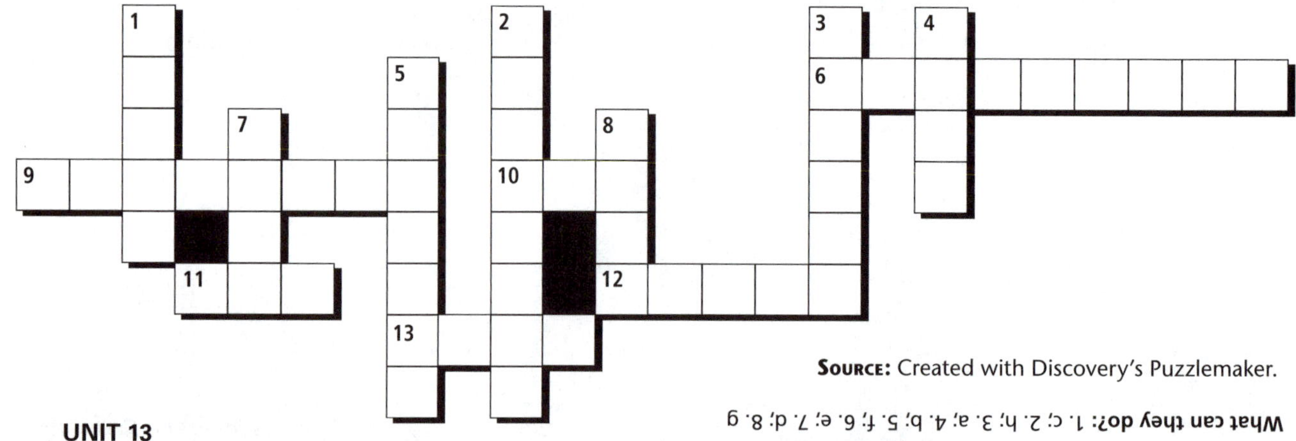

Source: Created with Discovery's Puzzlemaker.

What can they do?: 1. c; 2. h; 3. a; 4. b; 5. f; 6. e; 7. d; 8. g

UNIT 14

Life Events and Plans

LESSON 1

1 **Read about Yao Ming's life.**

Yao Ming's Life Story

Yao Ming was born on September 12, 1980. He grew up in a small apartment in Shanghai, China, with his parents. They were both basketball players, too—and tall! Their son is 2.26 meters (7 feet 5 inches). Yao doesn't have any brothers or sisters. When he was about nine, he went to the Youth Sports School in Shanghai. In China, he played for the Shanghai Sharks.

In 2002, Yao moved to the United States to play professional basketball. He plays for the Houston Rockets. When Yao first moved to Houston, he lived with his mother. Yao's mother cooked Chinese food for him, did the laundry, and cleaned their four-bedroom house.

Now look at the answers and write questions.

1. A: ______________________________? B: On September 12, 1980.
2. A: ______________________________? B: In Shanghai, China.
3. A: ______________________________? B: At the Youth Sports School.
4. A: ______________________________? B: In 2002.

2 **For each academic subject, write an occupation.**

1. architecture: ______________________
2. business: ______________________
3. medicine: ______________________
4. education: ______________________
5. engineering: ______________________

3 **Get to know a famous person's life story. Choose a famous person. Answer the questions. Use the Internet, books, and other sources for information.**

1. Person's name: ______________________________
2. When was he / she born? ______________________________.
3. Where was he / she born? ______________________________.
4. Where did he / she grow up? ______________________________.
5. What school did he / she go to? ______________________________.
6. What did he / she study? ______________________________.
7. Did he / she graduate? When? ______________________________.
8. What does he / she do now? ______________________________.

LESSON 2

4 **What are you going to do this summer? Check the boxes.**

☐ travel	☐ relax	☐ exercise
☐ go camping	☐ sleep late	☐ work
☐ go fishing	☐ do nothing	☐ go to school
☐ go bike riding	☐ hang out with friends	☐ move
☐ go to the beach	☐ go for walks	☐ go swimming

5 **Now write to a friend about your plans. Write sentences with <u>be going to</u>.**

6 **Answer the questions about your future plans with <u>be going to</u>.**

1. What are you going to do tonight? ______________________________.
2. What are you going to do tomorrow? ______________________________.
3. What are you going to do tomorrow night? ______________________________.
4. What are you going to do the day after tomorrow? ______________________________.

7 **Read the sentences. Ask yes / no questions with be going to.**

1. **A:** Rachel has a toothache.
   B: Is she going to see a dentist ____________________?
2. **A:** Jack doesn't feel well.
   B: ____________________?
3. **A:** I'm making chicken with rice, but there isn't any rice on the shelf.
   B: ____________________?
4. **A:** Anthony is going to travel to Europe.
   B: ____________________?
5. **A:** I don't have a clean shirt for work tomorrow.
   B: ____________________?
6. **A:** Julia is going to study medicine.
   B: ____________________?
7. **A:** We don't have any plans this weekend.
   B: ____________________?

LESSON 3

8 **Read about more events in Yao Ming's life.**

What's Next for Yao Ming?

In 2007, Yao Ming got married. His wife's name is Ye Li. Like Yao, she is tall (1.9 meters / 6 feet 3 inches) and a professional basketball player. She played for China in the 2004 Summer Olympics. Yao and Ye met in 1999 when they were teenagers. They were married in a small ceremony in Shanghai on August 6, 2007.

On May 12, 2008, there was a terrible earthquake in Sichuan Province, China. Yao and his wife started the Yao Foundation to help children in Sichuan. Yao's foundation is building new schools in Sichuan. Yao and Ye hope their foundation can also help children in other parts of China and in the U.S.

Now answer the questions.

1. What happened on August 6, 2007? ____________________.
2. What happened on May 12, 2008? ____________________.
3. What is the Yao Foundation doing now? ____________________
   ____________________.
4. What is the Yao Foundation going to do in the future? ____________________.
   ____________________.

9 **What would you like to do in your life? Write four sentences. Use the pictures and the verbs in the box for ideas.**

move	have children	meet
study	go	see
graduate	learn	buy
get married	travel	visit

Example: *I would like to travel to Australia*.

1. ______________________________.
2. ______________________________.
3. ______________________________.
4. ______________________________.

10 **Write two information questions with <u>would like</u> to ask each person.**

1. *When would you like to get married*?
2. ______________________________?

3. ______________________________?
4. ______________________________?

5. ______________________________?
6. ______________________________?

11 **A reporter from your school newspaper wants to write an article about you. Answer her questions about yourself.**

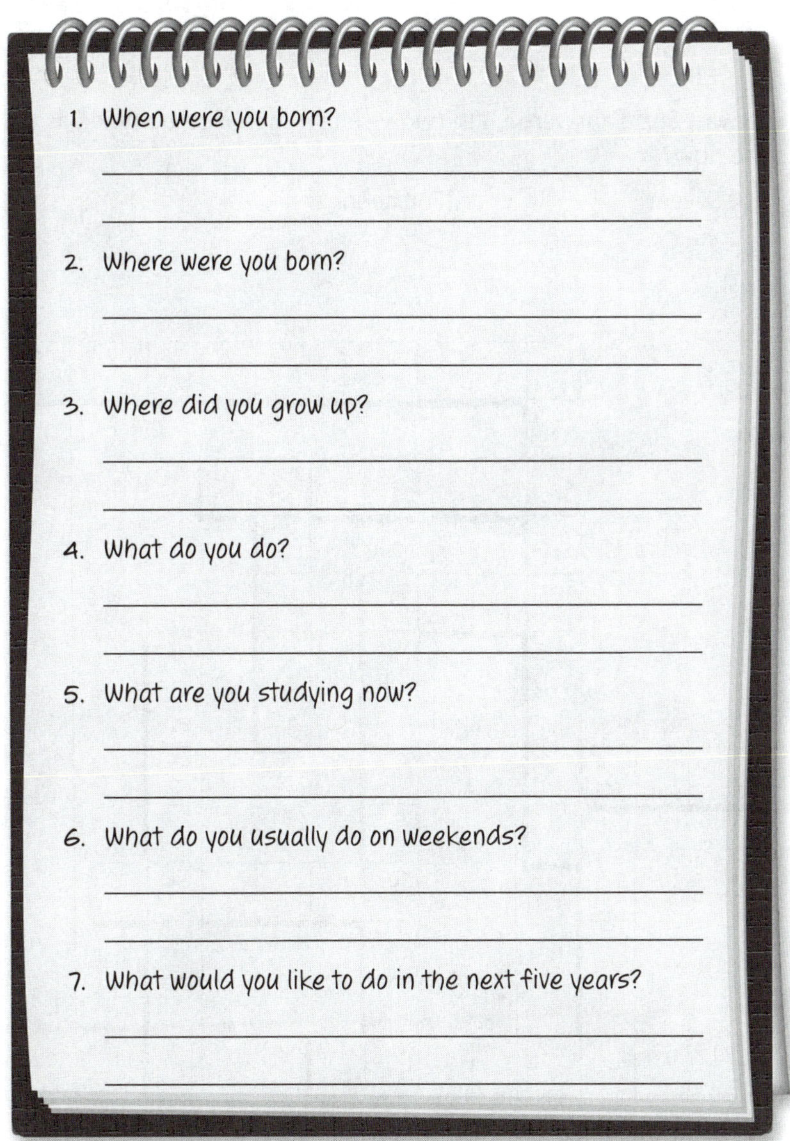

1. When were you born?
2. Where were you born?
3. Where did you grow up?
4. What do you do?
5. What are you studying now?
6. What do you usually do on weekends?
7. What would you like to do in the next five years?

JUST FOR **FUN**

A RIDDLE FOR YOU!

When asked how old she was, Suzie answered, "In two years I'm going to be twice as old as I was five years ago." How old is she now?

a. Twelve. **b.** Seven. **c.** Fourteen.

2 Complete the puzzle.

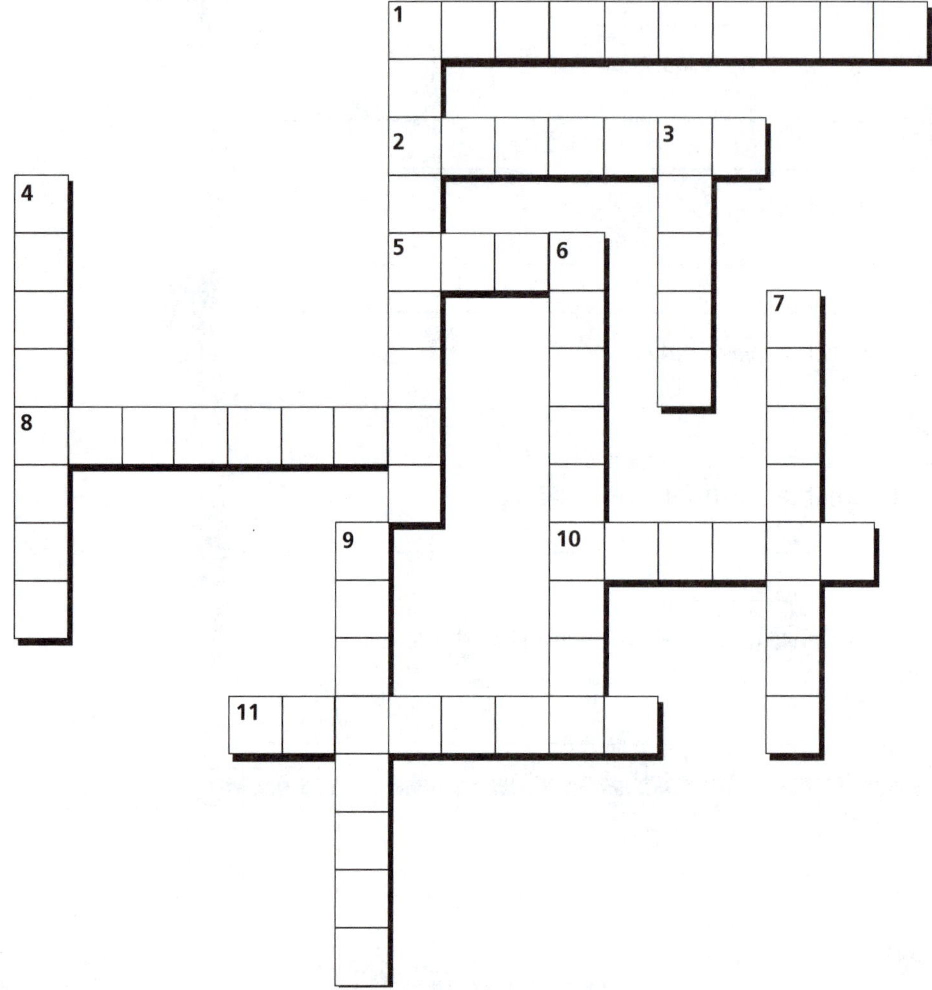

Across

1. Become husband and wife
2. Occupations
5. Go to live in a new home
8. Sons and daughters
10. Visit new cities
11. What future doctors study

Down

1. Sleep outdoors
3. Take a nap
4. Houdini's occupation
6. What future teachers study
7. Architecture, psychology, and law are all academic ______.
9. Complete school

Source: Created with Discovery's Puzzlemaker.

Riddle: a

UNITS 8–14

Review

1 **Answer the questions.**

1. Where do you live?

   ______________________________.

2. What's your home like?

   ______________________________.

3. How's the weather today?

   ______________________________.

4. What are you doing this weekend?

   ______________________________.

5. What do you have in your fridge?

   ______________________________.

6. What did you do last weekend?

   ______________________________.

7. What do you look like?

   ______________________________.

8. What can you do well?

   ______________________________.

9. Where were you born?

   ______________________________.

10. What would you like to do in the future?

    ______________________________.

2 **Complete the sentences. Use the correct verb form.**

1. Diane ______________ (go running) every day.
2. Alex ______________ (drive) to work right now.
3. We ______________ (cook) dinner for some friends last night.
4. I ______________ (relax) this weekend.

3 Read about Andrea Bocelli.

He's an opera singer from Italy, but people of all ages, young and old, listen to his music. He sings beautifully and is famous all over the world. He has wavy, gray hair. His name is Andrea Bocelli.

Bocelli was born on September 22, 1958, in Tuscany. He grew up on his family's farm. He started singing for family members when he was about three years old. When he was six, he learned to play the piano. He can also play the flute and the saxophone. At the age of twelve, he had a soccer accident, and now he can't see. Bocelli graduated from the University of Pisa. He studied law, but he worked for only one year as a lawyer.

What was next for Andrea Bocelli? He started to study music. His teacher was the famous singer Franco Corelli. In the evenings, he sang in piano bars to pay for his opera singing lessons. During this time, he got married. He and his first wife, Enrica, had two children, Amos and Matteo. In 1992, Luciano Pavarotti listened to a tape of Bocelli singing. That was the beginning of Bocelli's very successful career in music. Between 1994 and 2010, he made about 23 albums.

Bocelli lives in a pink house on the beach in Forte dei Marmi, Tuscany, not far from where he grew up. Bocelli studies music and practices singing for two hours or more every day. He travels a lot for his job. But he doesn't like to travel. He writes, too. He wrote a book about his life story, *The Music of Silence*. In his free time, he reads and cooks Italian food.

4 To write this article, a reporter interviewed Andrea Bocelli. Answer the reporter's questions for Bocelli.

1. **Reporter:** Where were you born?
   Bocelli: I was born in Tuscany.
2. **Reporter:** And did you grow up there?
   Bocelli: ______________________________.
3. **Reporter:** What did you study?
   Bocelli: ______________________________.
4. **Reporter:** Can you play any musical instruments?
   Bocelli: ______________________________.
5. **Reporter:** When did you learn to play the piano?
   Bocelli: ______________________________.
6. **Reporter:** Tell me about your family.
   Bocelli: ______________________________.
7. **Reporter:** Where do you live now?
   Bocelli: ______________________________.
8. **Reporter:** What's your typical day like?
   Bocelli: ______________________________.
9. **Reporter:** What do you do in your free time?
   Bocelli: ______________________________.

5 **Look again at the article in Exercise 3. Circle all 21 simple past tense verbs or past-tense forms of be in the article. Write 10 of these verbs on the lines. Then write the base form of the 10 verbs.**

1. was born → be born
2. ______ → ______
3. ______ → ______
4. ______ → ______
5. ______ → ______
6. ______ → ______
7. ______ → ______
8. ______ → ______
9. ______ → ______
10. ______ → ______

OPTIONAL VOCABULARY BOOSTER ACTIVITIES

1 **Check the items you have in your home. Then write which room they are in.**

1. ☐ intercom ______
2. ☐ fire escape ______
3. ☐ medicine cabinet ______
4. ☐ shower curtain ______
5. ☐ dishwasher ______
6. ☐ coffee maker ______
7. ☐ food processor ______
8. ☐ fax machine ______

2 **Go shopping for your home. What colors do you want? Write sentences.**

Example: sheets: I want gray sheets.

1. sheets: ______.
2. blanket: ______.
3. bath mat: ______.
4. towels: ______.
5. place mats: ______.
6. plates: ______.

3 **Circle the seasons where you live. Then complete the chart. Write the months and the weather in each season where you live.**

Seasons	Months	Weather
Spring		
Summer		
Fall		
Winter		

4 Make a fruit or vegetable salad. Write the ingredients on the recipe card.

______________ Salad

Ingredients:

5 Circle the word or phrase that is different.

1. grapefruit	(peach)	lemon	tangerine
2. fork	glass	teaspoon	knife
3. go sailing	go snorkeling	go windsurfing	go rock climbing
4. elbow	forehead	cheek	lip
5. saxophone	flute	trumpet	drums
6. biology	drama	medicine	chemistry

6 Check the activities that you do. Then circle your favorite activity.

_____ go rock climbing	_____ go hiking	_____ go snorkeling
_____ go rollerblading	_____ go ice skating	_____ garden
_____ play golf	_____ go sailing	_____ play soccer
_____ go skiing	_____ go horseback riding	_____ get a manicure

Now answer the questions.

1. How often do you do your favorite activity? ________________________________.
2. Where do you do your favorite activity? ________________________________.
3. Are you doing your favorite activity this month? When? ________________________________
________________________________.
4. Did you do your favorite activity last month? When? ________________________________
________________________________.
5. Which activity do you wish you could do? ________________________________.